D0456811

THE WALLS CAME TUMBLING DOWN

The Walls
Came Tumbling
Down

HENRIETTE ROOSENBURG

Foreword by Noel Perrin

A COMMON READER EDITION
The Akadine Press

The Walls Came Tumbling Down

A COMMON READER EDITION published 2000 by The Akadine Press, Inc.

A COMMON READER EDITION and fountain
colophon are trademarks of The Akadine Press, Inc.

ISBN 1-58579-004-4

10 9 8 7 6 5 4 3

To my friends Joke, Nell, Dries, and Jos,
and to all those who died so that Holland
might live.

Foreword

SOMETIMES human beings are hard to like. We are selfish, cruel, and greedy. We foul the earth. We exterminate or endanger other species, including some of the ones we most admire. (We've got world population of tigers down to about ten thousand, meanwhile increasing our own numbers by more than that every hour.) We are full of self-pity.

In an anti-heroic age such as the present, any sense of human niceness is especially hard to come by. Our literature—much of it, anyway—is devoted to deriding concepts like courage and self-sacrifice. Our biographers specialize in revealing that persons previously thought to be heroes had feet, ankles, and even thighs of clay—and were probably hollow to boot. Depressing.

Henriette Roosenburg's World War II memoir *The Walls Came Tumbling Down* is a splendid antidote to all this. Here is a book full of utterly unselfconscious heroism. Here is an author who shows in the most matter-of-fact way just how generous and brave human beings can be. She even shows, without particularly meaning to, that patriotism can be a solemn and lofty thing. It may be the last refuge of scoundrels, but under the right circumstances it is also the first thought of heroes.

Best of all, her story is both true and beautifully told. This is a book that many will weep as they read—I'm thinking of two passages in particular. But they will not be tears of sorrow. They will be hot tears of pride, pride that human beings can behave so nobly under such terrible circumstances. If you've never had the experience of catharsis, if maybe you've assumed it was just a fancy word that Aristotle liked to throw around, I confidently predict that reading this book will change your mind. Or has a good chance to, anyway.

Henriette Roosenburg, a middle-class Dutch girl with a fondness for literature, was a graduate student at the University of Leiden when World War II came along. She became a courier in the Dutch resistance movement, code name Zip. In 1944 she was caught by the Gestapo and promptly sentenced to death.

But the Nazis didn't immediately execute everyone they found guilty. Some they kept as prisoners, for possible killing (or work as a slave laborer) later.

Such prisoners were in a sense officially dead already, and they were universally known as the *Nacht und Nebel* or Night and Fog people. NNs formed the fourth and lowest class of prisoners to be found in a considerable number of German jails. The top class were German criminals—your ordinary rapist or thief. They got decent food, adequate medical attention, often a degree of power in running the prison. Next came black marketeers and other criminals from the occupied countries. They, too, generally got enough to eat.

Third were political prisoners, "ranging from the unfortunate innocent who had been denounced for listening to the BBC to the active resistance member who had been caught in an act of sabotage, of distributing an illegal newspaper, of sheltering Jews," or any other forbidden thing. The politicals were harshly treated, but they did have some rights, such as the right to go on sick call.

Finally came the *Nacht und Nebelen*, with no rights at all. Whenever enough cells were available, they were kept in solitary confinement. They got no mail, no medical attention, few amenities. (Zip was allowed to bathe three times during the eight months she spent in her final prison.) And they got so little food that most of the NNs weighed between 80 and 90 pounds.

On the day in May, 1945, when the walls tumbled down, there were 32 surviving female NNs, about half that many male ones, and hundreds of prisoners of the upper three classes. Five of the NNs are Dutch: three young women of whom Zip is one; an older woman, code name Fafa; and a young Dutch sailor named Dries. Dries got his death sentence for attempting to sail to England in a small boat in 1944.

Zip does not dwell on these matters, though. She is not writing a book about her sufferings in prison any more than she is about her heroism in the underground. (Her entire description of her job before she was caught is to mention casually that she transmitted information about German troop movements to London, "and occasionally helped Allied pilots when they happened to get stuck.") This is a book about what happened after the war ended and the walls crashed.

There is one exception. Zip does have a good deal to say about prison food, as she must, because the first great catharsis begins as a food riot.

The daily menu for third- and fourth-class prisoners runs like this. For breakfast, a slice of bread. For lunch, a bowl of thin soup. For dinner, another slice of bread, this time with an ounce of cottage cheese or ersatz jam. To be a little more cruel, or maybe just to save themselves bother, the guards gave out both slices of bread in the evening. By bitter experience, the prisoners learned that they had to save one slice for breakfast the next morning, or their hunger pangs were unendurable. Not easy to hold onto a slice of bread for twelve hours when you're starving.

It was the Russians who freed her. Their army came into the town of Waldheim, where the prison was, on May 6, 1945.

Russian soldiers go from cell to cell, unlocking. They do not release the female NNs, but that's only because the NNs are in so remote a part of the prison that the Russians don't know they're there. The third-class politicals know, though, and soon there's "a rush of wooden sandals on the staircase and shrill French voices shouting 'Les condamnés à mort!'" A minute later the NNs are free—and like every other starved prisoner in Waldheim they are tottering toward where they think the kitchens must be. At that moment the lights go out, and in the darkness pandemonium begins. There could have been a scene of mass trampling as the prisoners "mad with the first taste of freedom" and really almost crazed with hunger fought on toward the kitchens.

But at this moment one of the French politicals began to sing the *Marseillaise*. Henriette Roosenburg writes, "I have always loved the *Marseillaise*, and if ever I wanted to sing it, this was the moment. Yet I kept respectfully silent, for at the moment I felt they had an exclusive right to it."

Then, jammed there together in the dark, these starving people sang their national songs one by one: the Poles, the Czechs, the Belgians, the handful of Dutch. "It was the most solemn moment in my life, barring none. It was also the best thing that could have happened psychologically. It pulled us together, changed us from hungry animals into human beings with a purpose and a pride. The old spirit of the resistance, dulled and deadened by endless months of starvation and dehumanization, came alive again; the pushing and pulling stopped, and we were courteous to one another. In the darkness a hand came across and pushed a slice of bread into my hand. I said, 'No, no, keep it,' and a voice next to me whispered, 'No, it's yours. I stole it from your blanket.'"

In a few minutes the lights come back on, the prisoners begin liberating food and making flags, and the real action of the book begins. It is a true odyssey. This little group of Netherlanders is not free to go home, because the Russians are letting no one through their lines. The Poles and Czechs can and do go east to home; no one is going west.

Again, there is one exception. On the sixth day of their freedom, a miracle occurs. Word has somehow reached the west about these NNs and politicals, and a convoy of six U.S. Army trucks rumbles into Waldheim to rescue them. The Russians will occasionally wink at the no-crossing-the-line rule when it's fellow soldiers who want to cross.

There are more western prisoners than there is room in the trucks—even though you can get a lot of 80- and 90-pound adults onto one two-and-a-half-ton truck. Zip and the other young Dutch spotted the trucks early, and could easily have got on. They choose not to, even though the rumor has sprung up that the Russians are going to ship all the remaining westerners to a transit camp in Odessa. And why do they choose not to? Because Fafa, the older Dutch woman, has terrible arthritis—can't even stand up. Being an NN, she of course has had not so much as an aspirin in the last eight months. In no way is she up to a ride on shattered roads in the back of an army truck. They will not abandon her. They get her safely placed in a civilian hospital (no simple matter in the chaotic conditions of Europe in the spring of 1945), and only then do the four young ones begin the odyssey that is to take them back to the Netherlands.

They head for the river Elbe, where they hope to steal a boat. The first thing they find when they reach the river is a pair of Dutch barges trapped by broken bridges above and below. Their reception by the skippers of these two barges brought tears to my eyes, I suppose for the fourth or fifth time. It's *nice* to feel proud of human beings.

But you will find more than tearful scenes in this book. There's everything. There are scenes where Zip and the others have their chance for revenge on the prison guards and do or don't take it. There are scenes with the Russians that make you both love and get furiously exasperated with that mercurial people. There's even humor, such as the scene in a German house where they have pushed their way in to spend the night. One of the women in the house, herself a half-crazed refugee from British and American bombing, can't rest until she finds out which of the three young women Dries is sleeping with. The answer is none, in the sense that she means it. They have been too terribly starved. "None of us girls had menstruated for six months; Dries, after the first two nights of cuddling up close for lack of space, had confided that we didn't have to worry because, much as he loved the atmosphere, he couldn't have an erection."

But that answer would be unacceptable to the romantic housewife.

"All right, Zip," said Dries resignedly, "let's be married for one night, but let's tuck the girls in first."

When the book ends, Zip is home, and she is giving her mother a present. It's the one personal possession she had in prison: a six-inch square cut from her own underpants on which she had painstakingly embroidered a miniature history of her whole captivity. Many of the NNs who survived kept their sanity with secret and illegal embroidery—and there were times when a starving man would trade a scrap of his tiny food allowance for six inches of a particular color of thread.

Zip's mother collapses in tears. "You couldn't have done this," she sobs, "you never even knew in which hand to hold a needle."

This is a book that makes you realize that human beings can do practically anything. And it makes you glad we exist, glad the universe contains such creatures.

That scene with the embroidery took place in June, 1945. Henriette Roosenburg was 29 years old and an accomplished writer in both Dutch and English. Before the Gestapo caught her, she wrote for the Dutch underground newspaper *Het Parool* (*Free Word*). Her death sentence seems to have been as much for her illegal writing as for her illegal pilot rescues and courier work.

After the war she became a European correspondent for *Time* magazine, reporting from Paris and later from The Hague. In 1950 Time Inc. brought her to New York, where she lived for a decade. She was then already famous in The Netherlands. Among other things she had just become the first woman ever to receive the order of the Bronze Lion of the Netherlands.

During the first half of her stay in New York, Zip wrote what was to be her only book. It was an instant success. In 1956 *The New Yorker* published four long excerpts from it in four successive issues. For a writer that is even better than the Bronze Lion.

Zip died in 1972, at the relatively early age of 56. Those NNs who made it through the war often did die untimely. They had been through too much. But I do not think *The Walls Came Tumbling Down* will meet an untimely death. I think it has a long, long life still ahead. True heroism is irresistible.

Noel Perrin

THE WALLS CAME TUMBLING DOWN

Introduction

THIS is a story of the liberation of four Dutch political prisoners at the end of World War II, and about their trek home to Holland after Russian soldiers had freed them from the prison in Waldheim, a small village in south-eastern Germany. The four people are:

Nell, thirty years old. She was an official in the Netherlands scout movement whose organisational talents were extremely useful in the resistance. Until she was caught by the Gestapo in the autumn of 1943, she managed a network of hiding-places for Allied pilots who were shot down over Holland. She also had a hand in organising the Dutch end of an "escape line" running through Belgium and France to Spain and Portugal, with the purpose of getting these airmen back into action, where they would do the most good.

Joke (pronounced "Yokuh"), twenty years old. Barely out of high school, Joke threw herself wholeheartedly into working with a local resistance group, which concentrated on picking up shot-down Allied pilots in the moors around her village and finding hiding-places for them. She quickly graduated to a national movement and thus came to know Nell and other people on the "escape lines". She personally escorted several Allied airmen over the Dutch-Belgian border. Joke was caught in May 1944 and condemned to death.

7

Zip, twenty-eight years old, narrator of this story. As a student of Dutch and French literature at the University of Leiden, she began working in the "underground press" in the early days of the War, and eventually became a courier to Belgium, France, and Switzerland for a resistance group that transmitted intelligence about German troop movements and other matter to the Dutch government in London. As a courier she inevitably became entangled with some of the escape lines and occasionally helped Allied pilots when they happened to get stuck. In that way, she got to know both Nell and Joke. I was caught in March 1944 and condemned to death.

Dries, the lone man in the party, twenty-six years old. A merchant seaman, Dries happened to be on leave in Holland when the War broke out. In the spring of 1944 he tried, with three friends, to cross the English Channel, leaving from a Dutch beach. Foolhardy as the attempt was (for the Germans guarded the coast so well that it was impossible to launch a well-supplied and seaworthy craft) they were almost halfway before they found themselves surrounded by German warships and were ignominiously hauled back. Dries was thus caught in April 1944 and condemned to death.

The Nazis treated their political prisoners in various and hardly rational ways. Many prisoners were shot without trial. Many more were allowed to die from starvation, dysentery, tuberculosis, and other illnesses that were rampant in the concentration camps and prisons. Some, like the four in this story, were officially court-martialled, but their courts-martial were a parody of justice: the defence lawyer, appointed by the Nazis, wasn't allowed to see the prisoners before the sentencing. His only role was to be present while the sentence of death was pronounced—a pathetic reminder of the fact that Germany used to belong to the civilised nations and knew what the judicial process was.

Even after an official court-martial, the treatment differed.

Sometimes the condemned-to-death were taken out of the prison the next morning at dawn and shot at some convenient spot in the neighbourhood. Sometimes they were put in the so-called *"Nacht und Nebel"* (Night and Fog) group (called NN by both prisoners and guards) and shunted around from one prison to another, always farther away from the front lines. All four principals of this story belonged to the NN group.

Once inside the prisons or concentration camps, the NNs were the lowest category of prisoners. At the top were the German criminals, who got the coveted "trusty" jobs of distributing food and clothing (keeping the best of both for themselves) and working in the kitchens. Next came a medley of prostitutes, black marketeers, and petty criminals from all nations under German occupation. They were the assistants to the wardens, the runners of errands, the spies on the work details. The third category consisted of political prisoners, ranging from the unfortunate innocent who had been denounced for listening to the BBC to the active resistance member who had been caught in an act of sabotage, of distributing an illegal newspaper, of sheltering Jews or members of his underground group, or any of the thousand other acts that were *verboten* by the Nazis. These were the people who made up the work details. Their work could be anything from cutting wood in swamps to doing precision work on time fuses, from packing garbage to digging graves; it depended on what the camp or prison itself needed and the proximity of factories that were short of labour. These "politicals" had no privileges, no extra food or clothing. Their only advantage was an unintended one: they moved around, mingled with German workers or slave labourers in the factories they were assigned to, or, if they toiled in workshops inside a prison, with the criminals and prostitutes who distributed the daily tasks. They would sometimes get a German newspaper and read the news between the lines. Their grapevine was excellent and they usually lived, worked, and died in close-knit, loyal groups.

Next, and at the bottom of the pile, were the NNs. They

were kept in cells, and when they were led out for half an hour's exercise—about twice a week—special care was taken that no other prisoners should even see them. Some of the workshops had glass-topped doors facing the prison corridor. These were covered with black cloth whenever the NNs were led by to the exercise yard. Originally NNs were kept in solitary confinement; it was only in the last year of the War, when German prisons were crowded beyond belief, that this rule was relaxed—to the point where six NNs would be crowded into a one-person cell. The "politicals", if they were insistent enough and made enough noise, could complain to the head of the prison about bad food, inadequate quarters, stealing by the "trusties", etc; they did not always get results, but their complaints did help to prevent worse conditions. The NNs were expressly told that they had no right of appeal to anybody, and therefore were subject to more stealing of food by "trusties" and bad treatment from guards than anybody else.

This was the system for all prisoners (except for the Jews, who were sent to the extermination camps); in most of the big concentration camps it broke down in the last years of the War. The "trusties" proved too untrustworthy and the politicals, through their higher IQ and sheer weight of numbers, managed to capture the administration of the camps and most of the easier jobs. In the camps also, the dividing line between politicals and NNs often got lost.

But in the prisons we four went through, the system—except for the requirement of "solitary"—was rigidly enforced, and the NNs got the short end of every conceivable stick. After we three girls were moved from Holland to Germany, we spent eight months in five different German prisons. In some of them we stayed only a week or two before being moved on, in others three months or more. Yet in the entire eight months we had only three showers.

Prison routine for NNs was dreary in the extreme. A loud, persistent bell announced reveille at 5.30 a.m. About half an hour later a guard would come, open one cell, and allow two prisoners to come out, one with the toilet bucket, the other with the water jug. These two would cross over to the washroom on the other side of the wing, empty the bucket, fill the jug, and return. A second guard watched the washroom, so that we wouldn't leave any written messages there for other prisoners. She was highly unsuccessful, but that was our business. If the first guard was in a hurry, she would open the door of the second cell before the first two prisoners were locked in again, but any loitering or talking during this morning chore was quickly and severely punished, usually by kicking and beating, sometimes by withholding food.

At 8 a.m. the German criminal in charge of our food distribution would come round with a big jug of what was euphemistically called tea or coffee. The difference was in the colour of the water. If deep brown, it was a brew of pine cones and roasted sorghum and was called coffee. If greenish brown, it was made from some kind of herbs and called tea. The tea was far more palatable than the coffee. That was all there was for breakfast. Prisoners were supposed to keep one of the two slices of bread they were given every day, for their breakfast the next morning. Most of us eventually trained ourselves to do so, but ate it on awakening, long before the morning brew came around.

On weekdays the door would open again at 9 a.m. for the distribution of work. In Waldheim our work consisted of tearing goose feathers apart so that the down could be used for eiderdowns. Every day we would be given a big sack full of feathers and an empty sack for the down. Every day we would simply transfer the feathers from one sack to the other, pluck enough of them to cover the top of the sack with down, and call it a day. We hated the feathers, because even if we touched only the minimum needed to deceive the guards, the fluffy down would keep drifting around the cell, irritating our throats, settling in our food and water, and forming a perpetual health hazard for the many of us who had tuberculosis. Moreover, there was nothing one could do with feathers.

In Cottbus, the prison where we had spent three months before being sent to Waldheim, our job had been to take the knots out of old pieces of string. Much of the string had been used for baling hay and straw, and had quite obviously been lying around in farmyards and stables before it was collected and sent to the prisons: it came to us full of dried manure, dirt, vermin, and an occasional grain of wheat or rye—which we would carefully pry loose and eat, chewing on it as long as we could before swallowing. We never found out what the Nazis wanted to do with all the untied string they hoped to collect from us, but we loved the string for its endless possibilities. We plaited it and then sewed it together to make such things as double-soled sandals for our cold feet, broad belts to keep our waists warm, small Disney-like animals to give to fellow NNs at Christmas, bread-baskets to cheer up the monotony of our cell furniture. Every once in a while the guards would search our cells while we were in the exercise-yard and take away all the treasures that we didn't carry on our persons or hadn't hidden well enough inside the cells. But since there was always more string available, we would patiently set about replacing the stolen objects. Eventually we even obtained extra food by selling the German "trusties" one pair of sandals for six potatoes and two slices of bread.

But the feathers in Waldheim defied us. We tried to make flowers out of them, but we had nothing to dye them with, and they were too fragile to last. Occasionally we would gather some of the longest quills and play a game of "jack straws" with them, but on the whole we considered the feathers a frightful nuisance. Our main distractions in Waldheim, therefore, were our various embroideries and the endless talk about food that is common to all starving prisoners.

Embroidery, or any personal activity, for that matter, was forbidden and had to be done on the sly. Yet through all those long, trying months it proved to be one of our greatest life-savers. In one of the first prisons where I was confined, I had been forced to mend uniforms and socks for the German Army.

The mending was never satisfactorily done, but I obtained two needles which I kept till the very end. One was very thin but had a reasonably big eye. It was my favourite, and I never let it out of my sight. The other was slightly thicker; I would either lend it to good friends such as Nell and Joke, or exchange it, for a limited time, with other prisoners against such treasures as coloured bits of thread or the use of a pair of scissors.

From the very beginning I also managed to hold on to a square linen handkerchief of my father's that I happened to have when I was caught. As time went on, this piece of linen became more and more valuable, for as I passed through each prison I embroidered in small characters the name, my cell number, and dates, plus, in a half-circle around them, the song we associated with that particular jail, and some microscopic drawings of the things that happened to us. To give an example: Nell, Joke, and I spent ten days in a prison near Aachen, called Anrath. We were in "solitary", but our cells were adjacent, and we conversed by tapping Morse signals on the walls. On my precious handkerchief the name Anrath, the cell number, and the dates (September 8–17, 1944) are duly noted. So are Joke's and Nell's names in Morse, indicating both the "solitary" and the fact of communication. Between those is a crude drawing of a gun (in field-grey thread pulled out of uniforms I was supposed to mend) to convey the fact that we heard what we thought was Allied gunfire. Around it all is the song "We don't Know Where We're Going Until we're There" —very apt, as it turned out.

By the time we reached Waldheim, most of the NNs in our group had some kind of embroidery under way. We had almost as many needles as prisoners. We had one pair of scissors among our six cells, and we would pounce on any rag, no matter how small, and make something out of it. When spring came and we no longer feared the cold of the unheated cells so much, we cheerfully cut small squares out of our tattered underwear and changed them into the most complicated works of art. A Frenchwoman in my cell was a wizard at "open-seam" work and taught me patiently. When I thought I had mastered the art, I cut a six-by-six-inch piece out of my cotton panties (the largest whole square I could find) and embroidered it into an intricate network of spiderwebs.

The search for coloured thread for our embroideries never stopped. White thread was easy: one just pulled it out of white underwear, or sheets or towels, if any. An inch at a time would do; we had time and patience enough to pull an inch of thread through, disengage the needle, insert the needle as far as it would go, insert the thread again, pull it through, repeat the process, and secure the minuscule tail of thread that was left. Black was equally easy to obtain, for most of us had been issued with black cotton uniforms. So was yellow, for every NN wore a yellow sleeve band. Any other colour was precious, the object of intense bargaining.

One of the NNs, an elderly Belgian woman who had sheltered Allied pilots, had managed, by extremely loud and persistent protests about a kidney ailment, to keep her girdle. At the end of her imprisonment the girdle certainly didn't support her kidneys; it flapped as loosely around her as any of the issued clothing. Yet the girdle may have helped to keep her alive; for whenever any of us needed any pink for the embroidery we had in mind, she would craftily trade a short length of pink thread for a crust of bread, half a potato, or some spoonfuls of soup.

The truth is that the human body can stand much more starvation than we commonly suppose, as long as the human mind has something, no matter how trivial, to fasten upon. In this case the girdle-owner concentrated her mind on the trade for food, actually acquired some extras, and survived. The rest of us concentrated on our embroideries and, although starving, could bring ourselves to trade scraps of food for pink thread. Many NNs died before the end of the war, but never because of such trading. As far as I have seen, they died either from incurable illnesses induced by starvation (such as tuberculosis) or filth (such as typhoid fever) or by plain torture, or sin͟ͅ because their minds were too tired to carry on the fight. I have seen people lie down and die within a few days after their spirit gave up. Some of them were religious, some were not. The lesson I learned was that people can hang on to life through the most atrocious circumstances if they can find something outside themselves to concentrate on—even if it is only a poor square of cotton or a pink-threaded girdle.

By May 1945 all the NNs interested in embroidery had a small cache of multicoloured thread that they traded with one another. I remember my joy when, during one dreary round in the exercise-yard, I suddenly spotted a piece of delicately twisted string, brown and yellow, about twenty inches long. I pretended to faint then and there, grabbed the string, and lay quiet for about ten minutes, letting the guard kick me. Once untwisted, the threads of the string were soft as silk, and the brown as well as the peculiar shade of yellow proved eminently exchangeable against some red and blue that I needed. The only thing that worried me afterward was that Joke really believed in my collapse and kept saving for me some of the food she badly needed herself. It took a week to convince her!

At noon we were served soup made of grated rutabagas and water, with sometimes a vague taste of lard or meat, every other vestige of which had been carefully extracted before the soup pails reached the NNs. Every prisoner was theoretically entitled to one litre (slightly less than a quart) of soup, and the bowls were made accordingly. But whenever ours were filled to the rim, we had a celebration—it happened so rarely. Once every two weeks or so we would get six small and usually rotten potatoes and half a litre of soup. Those were great days, for potatoes had good filling power, and so did the odds and ends of peels and sprouts that we managed to grab with our servings.

Sometimes, in the afternoon, we were taken out for a half-hour walk around the exercise-yard. More often we were simply left in our cells. At 4 p.m. every prisoner was handed two half-inch-thick slices of dark bread and a one-ounce container of ersatz jam, cottage cheese, sugar, or, very rarely, lard. At 7 p.m. there was another trip to the washroom, then a roll-call by numbers, for NNs were strictly nameless. After that we were left alone for the night.

Next to our embroideries, however, there was another occupation to which we devoted considerable energy and imagination: the ceaseless quest for news from the outside.

Every prison had its small hospital and medical department. The NNs, however, were denied the regular sick call. Weeks of complaining and needling would go by before a guard would grudgingly take an NN over to the hospital. Paradoxically, only the strongest could risk the trip. This we discovered in winter, when a Danish woman was finally allowed to go for medical treatment after weeks of high fever and coughing blood. She died while waiting in line in the freezing rain outside the hospital door. Yet the waiting-line at the hospital was an excellent source of news; Joke, Nell, and I would take turns trying to get there, just for that reason. There was no need for trumped-up sicknesses; all of us had dysentery and festering sores on our bodies that wouldn't heal because we never got the necessary nourishment.

Our next-best source of news was a group of French politicals who were given half an hour of exercise in the yard below our windows about five times a week, and who would chant or shout bits of news and gossip whenever they were far enough away from a guard. Our windows were set high in the wall, about six feet from the floor. There were bars on the inside and opaque glass on the outside. The glass part could be opened to an angle of about forty-five degrees by a vertical steel bar attached to the wall. The only way of looking out was to climb up by way of the single stool that every cell possessed, hang on to the bars and, with the window opened as far as possible, crane one's neck around the transom. Looking out was strictly *verboten*, and we could be caught both by the guards outside glancing up, or by the silent spies that were always shuffling along the corridors and watching our activities through the peep-holes set in the heavy wooden doors of our cells. The penalty was three days without food for everybody in the cell.

This penalty was so formidable and so dangerous (starved people can die very quickly when they are denied any food at all) that the risk of looking out was taken only after considerable discussion and with majority consent in every cell. There were thirty-six NNs in this prison, crammed together in six cells. By common consent the risk was divided over the cells, every cell taking its turn. A prisoner develops an uncanny sixth sense for knowing when he is watched; we would draw our heads back the instant before the guard outside decided to look up; we would drop down from the bars and continue our task of tearing goose feathers apart, the very second before the lid on the peep-hole was silently lifted. We spent three and a half months in this particular prison, and we managed to make contact with the French politicals almost every day they were out in the yard. Yet only two cells had the dreadful punishment inflicted on them. One of them was mine, and I was the culprit. The guards in the yard had not seen me, but, unknown to me, the doctor had been watching from a window of the hospital. This so-called doctor, a maniacal sadistic virago, came rushing over to our wing to assure herself personally that orders for our punishment were given. To her it made absolutely no difference if the inmates under her care died from starvation—as long as the rules were enforced. It is no wonder that her hospital was more frequently called the death house.

During the last three weeks before the liberation the prison had been buzzing with rumours. "The Rhine has been crossed" —this one we had heard so often that we didn't dare believe it any more. "President Roosevelt has died"—this one we discounted as Nazi-inspired. "The Russians are only fifty miles away"—that seemed more probable. Three months earlier we had been moved from Cottbus, east of Berlin, because the Red Army was close to the German-Polish border. At that time we could hear the bridges to the east being blown up and we had

B

shared the cattle cars that took us south with groups of Polish prisoners from the several towns in Poland that had been evacuated on orders from the retreating German armies. As a matter of fact, we had spent the time wondering what took the Red Army so long.

Then, one night in late April, shells had come whistling over the prison. We lay huddled in the dark, listening to the muffled firing of guns somewhere in the distance, the high-pitched shriek of the shells as they seemed to brush the roof over our heads, and the loud explosions that followed. We listened, counted, and hoped—hoped that this was *it*, that we would wake up free, that the prison wouldn't be hit. After about an hour the shelling stopped; nothing else happened, and when we woke up the next morning, we were still prisoners. But from that day on the prison hospital flew a Red Cross flag.

The next rumour was a thoroughly disquieting one: "The Nazis are freeing all the criminals, and they're going to shoot all the NNs." After we had been liberated ourselves, we found that this rumour, like all the others of that last month, had been entirely true: criminals were sent home from many German prisons just before the collapse, and Himmler *did* give an order that all condemned-to-death prisoners were to be shot. The order did not reach all prisons and camps in time, and in some, like ours, it wasn't carried out—maybe because there was no firing-squad handy. In others, however, it was. In Halle, for example, several NNs, two Dutchmen among them, were executed two days before the town was liberated.

For ten long days we had to live with this intelligence as best we could. Every time we heard the ugly jangling of keys in the corridor, we held our breath. Were they coming to shoot us? It was not a new sensation, for we had known it in the months just after our court-martial and before we had become part of the NN group. Since then we had become more and more intent on survival, and once in a while we would do some cheerful speculating about the reasons for the existence of the NN group: surely, if they had kept us this long, it meant that we were intended as exchanges against some high-ranking Nazis who were prisoners of the Allies; or again, they might use us as a bargaining-point in obtaining conditions of surrender; and so on. Yet now, while we were more than ever convinced that the end of the war was just around the corner, the spectre of the firing-squad was with us again, gnawing at our daylight thoughts and haunting our uneasy sleep.

Chapter One

MAY 6, 1945, was a day of foreboding. It was a Sunday; reveille was half an hour later than on weekdays. This was routine, but the guard who came to open our doors was not. She was a young blowsy woman we had never seen before, and she opened all six NN cells at once, without seeming to care how many prisoners left each cell. Moreover, she was alone; the usual guard at the washroom was absent. In no time at all, all thirty-two NNs (there had been thirty-six when the group arrived in Waldheim but four of our number had died) had poured into the corridor and were happily milling around, talking excitedly to old friends from other cells, darting over the narrow crosswalk that led over the stair-well to the washroom, and searching around there for messages or for rags that could be used for embroidery.

The guard then proceeded to do another unprecedented thing: she crossed the stair-well and opened the five cells opposite ours (the sixth was the washroom). It proved how new she was, for two of the cells were untenanted. She peeked in and closed them again. We had never known anything about these prisoners opposite us, even though we did have contacts with many others from unknown parts of the prison. Any prisoner, political or criminal, can tell you that a stair-well is one of the hardest sound-barriers to cross: the sound goes down before it can get across and therefore inevitably reaches a guard before it reaches a prisoner. We knew from previous experience that

the results could be extremely uncomfortable for all cells concerned, and we had never tried to reach our opposite numbers.
They must have taken their exercise in a different yard from the
one below our windows, for we never saw them there.

Yet this Sunday morning we recognised them as soon as they
appeared in the corridor. They were fourteen of the twenty-two
Polish politicals who had shared with us the cattle car that
had brought us from Cottbus to Waldheim, a journey of eighty
miles that had taken two days and three nights without food or
water. The Polish women came dancing into the washroom and
embraced us like long-lost sisters, babbling excitedly in their
own language, which none of us could understand. But their
sign language was unmistakable; they kept pointing at the
doors and throwing their arms wide, then pointing at us and
making running movements. And all the time they laughed and
shook our hands. It was quite obvious that they thought it
wouldn't be long before we would all get out of there. We
responded with a pantomime of the good things that would
be coming to us—mostly gestures of eating, smoking, and
yawning ease. I tried to learn the Polish words for these occu-
pations, but the general confusion was too great; all I caught
was a sound like *"papiroski"* for "cigarettes", which I filed
away for future reference. The bedlam lasted for about half an
hour before sharp voices from the main floor caused our nonchalant guard to detach herself from the stair-rail she had been
leaning on and herd us back to our cells. We were grateful to
this newcomer and made no trouble, but just before I stepped
back into my cell Nell brushed past me and said, "Fafa is in the
next wing." Then the door closed.

My cellmates at that time were three Frenchwomen and one
Belgian. We arranged our bedding—consisting of two sacks
filled with wood shavings—and ourselves around the cell and
indulged in excited speculation while we gnawed on the one
slice of bread we had kept from the day before and waited for
the morning brew. For myself, I reflected on Nell's terse bit of
information. Fafa was a Dutch political with whom we had had

close contact in Cottbus and who had been transported to
Waldheim with us. By that time she had already been badly
crippled with arthritis, and we had often feared for her life during these last three months, for none of our efforts to communicate with her again had succeeded. But now Nell seemed to
know where she was, which meant first of all that she was alive.

The excitement of the early morning lasted till the ersatz
coffee was distributed. In our secret hearts we must all have
expected something startling to happen at the next opening of
doors; when nothing did, our *soufflé* of high hopes collapsed
into gloom. After a while we got out our embroideries and,
sitting on the one stool, the floor, the two piled-up mattresses,
shoulders hunched away from the peephole to protect our work
from the ever-prying eyes, we worked away silently at our
piteous fantasies in bits of colour. I was experimenting with a
new stitch, which I hoped would make a branch of gladioli
more lifelike, but my heart wasn't in it. I kept straining my ears
till I felt I could hear the pulse and the breathing of every
prisoner in the building, and I was almost glad when Mickey,
the youngest among us, said out loud what I had been trying
to ban from my thoughts: "Maybe they let us fool around
because we're going to be shot today."

To my own surprise I found I had the answer ready: "Have
you ever known them to be that considerate? Don't be silly.
They're getting disorganised themselves, that's all. Come on,
let's sing."

We sang several French songs, and the atmosphere in the
cell improved a little; yet the morning seemed interminable,
and long before the appropriate time we had started making
extravagant predictions about what the noon meal would consist of. From there we drifted, as usual, into talk about the
most fanciful menus, and Laure, a spunky middle-aged Frenchwoman whose throat was horribly swollen from tuberculosis of
the glands, kept us spellbound for a while with a succulent
description of roast duck with oranges and all the trimmings.
When the food finally arrived the disappointment was all the

more painful; instead of the slightly thicker soup, with some beans or peas in it, that we counted on for Sundays, it was the usual thin orange slop, scraped rutabagas and water. There was a highly unusual fillip, however. The distribution was done by a team of three: a guard who unlocked the door; the German criminal, a mean-eyed murderess, who was our usual supervisor and who swung the ladle; and Joke, who dragged the pails along our six doors. I was the last to hold up my bowl; Joke bent down with her face close to mine, hissed "Hitler is dead," and dragged the pail away. The door closed.

Amidst the swearing over the poor thin soup I had some trouble communicating this latest bit of gossip, but when it penetrated, the whole cell burst out laughing. I don't think any of us really believed it, but it was too good not to savour and gloat over and turn into wild fantasies. As usual the soup did not still our hunger in the least, but our minds were so busy with the added titbit that we hardly noticed it. We spent a hilarious hour discussing the most horrible deaths for Hitler, and we made up a long list of Nazi bigwigs who we were sure had died with him, including all the Gestapo agents we had had to deal with and all the representatives of Nazi power in our various countries. After a while I stood under the window and sang a Dutch song, as loudly as I dared. Nell picked it up in the next cell, and pretty soon we could hear Joke's voice from three cells away. I stopped then, and so did Nell; both of us could hear Joke carrying on the tune but changing the words to: "It's true, he's dead, I heard it from——" She broke off abruptly and we knew there was danger near and hurried to hide our embroideries.

But the danger turned out to be a surprise: we were being taken out for exercise, an unheard-of-thing on a Sunday. Again there was but one guard instead of the usual three, and once we were in the yard, she let discipline break down completely. We had always been required to walk singly and without speaking, keeping two yards' distance between each other and holding our hands behind our backs. Since one guard wasn't enough to enforce these rules, she hardly tried. Joke, Nell, and I were soon walking abreast, and they filled me in on the background of their news. Joke had heard hers from one of the prisoners of the kitchen detail who brought the soup pails up to our floor—an unusual thing in itself, for as a rule Joke was not let out of her cell till the kitchen detail had left. And in the morning, while the rest of us had been aimlessly walking around, Nell had had the presence of mind to dart into the next wing and lift the peep-hole covers of one cell after another, looking for Fafa. She had found her, but when she knocked on the door and made her presence known, another prisoner had come to talk to her. Fafa had stayed where she was, huddled in a corner under a blanket. "Apparently she's so crippled she can't move at all," said Nell. "We'll have to get her out when they come to liberate us."

"When they come to liberate us"—but would they ever come?

Toward four, the evening food came around: two slices of bread and a paper-thin slice of sausage apiece. It was the first meat we had seen in a long time. We put one slice of bread away for the morning, ate the other slice, sucked on the sausage till it dissolved into nothingness, and waited again. Waited for what? For the next day? For liberation? For death? We didn't know.

There was no roll call that night. The church clock near by boomed out seven, then seven-thirty, and still no roll call. At eight we decided to get ready for the night. We spread our two mattresses next to each other, then bedded down on them crosswise, the only way that the five of us could fit onto them. Our feet dangled over the edges, but at least each of us had two inches of wood shavings between her bony body and the concrete floor. We wrapped ourselves in the blankets we had been issued after the winter was over, and wriggled ourselves into our usual jigsaw puzzle of limbs and shoulders and hips. But we couldn't sleep. The prison was alive. There was noise from all directions—unrecognisable, unaccountable noises, the stirrings of thousands of prisoners asking themselves why there had been no roll call and hoping, hoping. . . . Lying awake and listening, I thought it sounded like a storm in the woods in the first days of spring: branches sigh and creak, oak-trees rustle with a last mantle of dead leaves, and rain comes rushing through like a deep breath, full of promise and bursting force.

I found myself trembling and sat up. Nobody was asleep. "Do you mind if I look out?" I asked humbly.

They did mind. Laure scolded me gently: "You've kept me alive all this time—what do you want to kill me for now?" There was a special bond between Laure and me; every day I had patiently pressed the pus out of her infected throat glands and kept the wound opening as clean as I could under the circumstances. I knew she was right: after another punishment of three days without food none of us might survive.

Mickey, who slept next to me, was trembling too. "I wish something would happen," she groaned. "I can't stand this much longer." We all knew that Mickey would sometimes grow hysterical and break out into wild sobbing or screaming fits. Already feeling guilty for having disturbed our general effort to sleep, I gave in and lay down again.

On the other side of Mickey, Jeanne wormed her body around in the little space she had, put an arm around the young girl, and started soothing her, saying, "There now, baby, it can't be long now. Something will happen. You go to sleep. Maybe tomorrow they will come."

We kept quiet for about an hour, but none of us went to sleep. We were all listening, waiting, feeling the tension of the whole prison, trying to keep our own tension under control. I knew by the church clock that nine-thirty had passed when I became aware of other noises coming from the town. There was a single shout. There were some far-off rifle shots; then more shouts; then a kind of rumbling that seemed to swell but never became distinct enough to be recognisable. I sat up, undid my blanket, and said loudly, "This time I'm going to look out."

Laure laughed and said, "Go ahead, it's almost dark anyway,

they won't see you from the outside." Mickey and Jeanne agreed also. Only Dora, the Belgian woman, was still against it, but she was overruled.

I got the stool, placed it on top of the mattresses, climbed on, and pulled myself up to where I could rest one knee in a dent in the wall made exactly for that purpose. There was a shimmer of daylight left, but the stars and the moon were out. My eyes were enough accustomed to the dark to see quite clearly: there was the yard, the prison wall, the roofs of buildings outside the wall, and beyond them the few yards of sloping street coming down a hillside, our only glimpse of "normal" life. I concentrated on that bit of street now, just faintly discerning the whitish line of its pavement against the dark walls of the houses that lined it. There was nothing to see. My hands hurt around the bars, my knee hurt against the rough cement. I was almost ready to drop down, defeated, when the miracle happened: a lighted bus lurched down my little bit of street. It not only had headlights, it was lighted up inside, and I could distinguish a few vague forms inside it before it disappeared between the buildings. One has to have lived through five years of blackout to imagine the utter incongruity of a bus with lights inside and out. I dropped back in such haste that I kicked over the stool and landed on top of Mickey.

"They're here!" I shouted. "They're here, I just saw them, there was a big bus with all its lights on!"

Catching my excitement, the others all scrambled up and pressed me for details. "Are they Russians?" "Are they Americans?" "Who are they?" "How do you know?"

"I don't know who they are, but they're here, in a lit-up bus, I tell you!"

Just then there were some more shouts outside, and, suddenly and clearly, the sound of a revving motor. "That's them," I yelled. "You hear them? That's my bus!" I banged on the wall to get Nell in the next cell. As soon as she banged back I started tapping in Morse, "Bus with lights." She tapped back, "Where?" Too excited for this slow Morse conversation, I gave her the signal to come to the window, scrambled up again myself, and found that I had an audience at all windows. I shouted the news in French and Dutch for all to hear, and excitement ran through the wing like wildfire.

My cellmates had picked up the mattresses and leaned them against the wall; now we were standing in the dark cell, each clutching a blanket, a slice of bread, and the embroideries. The noise in the prison swelled to a mighty roar, wave following wave, around us, near us, yet not near enough. We were still locked in. Were they forgetting us? In furious frustration we banged on the doors, tried to kick out the panels; then there it was: a rush of wooden sandals on the iron staircase and shrill French voices shouting, *"Les condamnés à mort, les condamnés à mort!"* The French politicals had not forgotten us; they were coming to our rescue. There was an unbearable moment while we heard doors being opened, screams and shouts from prisoners rushing out; then the jangle of keys was at our door, the door was open, and we burst into a throng of Frenchwomen and one thin Russian soldier who had the keys. We smothered him with greetings; he pushed us off patiently and went on to the next cell, still guided by some of the Frenchwomen.

I remember being pushed against the rail of the stair-well and standing there stock-still, watching this slight young fellow in a drab tunic going about the business of liberation. He opened the next cell and again was almost buried under an avalanche of five gaunt females who hugged him and kissed him and tore at his clothes. Again, patiently and gently, he brushed them off, like so many importuning kittens, and went on to the next cell to encounter the same onslaught. He would soon turn the corner now and go into the next wing. I suddenly felt I couldn't bear it, I couldn't lose him—not yet. Pushing my way through the throng I got to him just as he was ready to insert his keys into the lock of the last cell on our block. The same force that had propelled me to him made me take off his cap, rip off the Red Army star, and put the cap back on his head. He had one hand on the keys and with the other he started to grab for his star. Then he saw my face, or at least something in it, for he shrugged and smiled. I kissed him full on the lips. He turned the key, and that was the last I saw of him.

I made my way back to look for Nell and Joke and found them still near their own cells, each clutching a rolled-up blanket, not quite out of the shock, jabbering away with some of the French politicals who had brought us our liberator. I felt as if I was beginning to function again, but wasn't too sure, and my first words to them were harsh: "Hey, we better get organised. That corner cell opposite us is empty. Can you get Fafa there? I'll go for food and——" The rest was lost, for they came out of their daze and we looked at each other and realised that here we were, all three of us, alive and free! We fell into each other's arms and hugged and kissed, and the first tears came, and the first sobs of happiness.

All this time the lights had been on in the stair-well and corridors, although not in the cells, but just when the three of us were making our first adjustment to freedom, all lights went off and the scene of utter confusion was unexpectedly plunged into darkness. There followed a few seconds of near-panic. Roars and screams came up from the lower floors, and we suddenly realised that we were tightly packed among scores of prisoners, all of them mad with the first taste of freedom, and all of them surging for the stairs in complete blackness, for the windows of the stair-well were pasted over with black paper. But the French, God bless them, rescued us again. A voice rang out with the "*Marseillaise*" and everybody stood still while all the Frenchwomen around us joined in and the rousing song echoed from the damned prison walls. I have always loved the "*Marseillaise*" and if ever I wanted to sing it, this was the moment. Yet I kept respectfully silent, for at the moment I felt that they had an exclusive right to it. Or maybe my throat was too full of tears; I don't know. Yet when our turn came the Dutch "*Wilhelmus*" rang out just as valiantly, and I put all my enthusiasm into it. The Poles followed, then the Belgians. It

was the most solemn moment in my life, barring none. It was
also the best thing that could have happened psychologically.
It pulled us together, changed us from hungry animals into
human beings with a purpose and a pride. The old spirit of the
resistance, dulled and deadened by endless months of starvation and dehumanisation, came alive again; the pushing and
pulling stopped and we were courteous to one another. In the
darkness a hand came across and pushed a slice of bread into
my hand. I said, "No, no, keep it," and a voice next to me
whispered, "No, it's yours, I stole it from your blanket, I'm
sorry." I took the bread and started eating it. I knew the voice
had spoken the truth, and when later I unrolled my blanket, I
was glad to find my souvenirs and embroideries, and didn't
even look for the bread.

After the catharsis of the national anthems, the lights were
still off, but our eyes had become used to darkness again and
there was enough moonlight coming through the open doors of
the cells to enable us to make out people and other forms. Nell,
Joke, and I talked over our next move; they both decided that
my first breathless plan had been all right. They would try to
move Fafa to the corner cell, and I would go down and try
to get food and news. I gave them my blanket for safe keeping
and moved toward the stairs. Almost everybody else was
moving towards those stairs too, yet the movement was orderly
till we got down to the second floor. There we were joined by
a sudden thrust of prisoners from that floor, who apparently
had just been given their freedom and had not had time to get
over their shock. They had heard our singing, however, for
when I landed, bruised and buffeted, at the bottom of the
stairs, a voice asked, "Was it you who sang?" I gasped, "Yes,"
and I could hear the voice saying "Thank you" as its owner
was carried away in a stream of prisoners.

Here I was on the main floor, in a hysterical throng surging
around in the darkness. Even with lights I would have had a
hard time finding my way to the kitchens, for I knew no more
about the layout of the prison than what I had been able to

learn from our occasional walk to the exercise yard, and we had never passed the kitchens. I could only struggle along with the main stream, hoping that somebody knew where we were all going. I had no doubt that the main stream would be heading for food. My main concern was to keep my bearings so that I would know how to get back to Nell and Joke. We turned one corner to the left. The movement was as slow as that of a great crowd at a coronation, but it was much more frightening because of the darkness and because every human being here had a furious pulse in her own blood, not quite rational, not quite sane, made up of an extreme desire for physical freedom, of animal hunger, and of a multitude of only half-realised, contradictory feelings. Everybody seemed to be yelling and roaring at once, yet I was aware of many silent persons struggling along with me. There were snatches of conversation: "How far are we from the main exit?" "I don't know. Aren't we going to to kitchens?" "Yes, of course." But then the contact would be lost and the questioning would start anew, left and right.

I knew that by now we had passed the turn-off where our little group of NNs had been herded to the yard, and that I was in strange territory. There seemed to be a faint light ahead, and the crowd picked up speed. We turned another corner and the light became real; it came from a crude torch of rags attached to a rifle which hung away from a wall by a short piece of wire. In its light at least ten couples, all consisting of Russian soldiers and prisoners, were making love on the floor of the corridor. I had made my way near enough to the head of the crowd to get a glimpse of this obstacle in our way. In the next second the ranks closed and we surged over them. I never knew whether they managed to get up fast enough to avoid being trampled to death. There was no time to worry, for the crowd had turned another corner and was now streaming down a staircase toward a lighted doorway which turned out to be the kitchen entrance. The kitchens were located in the basement and obviously had their own generator, for here all the electric lights were blazing. It was also obvious that we were not the first wave to get down here. We came into a big room where there had been tables and chairs, now all smashed to pieces, and which had several doors. I noticed one in particular, because it seemed to give onto the outside; there was a blackout curtain in front of it that was swinging on the wind.

On the other side of the room was a well-organised battle-line of the kitchen detail. There was not a guard in sight, yet these well-fed criminals were obviously determined to pass out their stores as parsimoniously as they could. They were lined up four deep in front of what was plainly their storeroom, and they had a barrier of broken furniture in front of them. The minute they saw our crowd bursting in, they started handing out loaves of bread and very small containers (three ounces at most) of lard, shouting all the while, "One to a person, one to a person, there isn't enough of it, leave something for the others, will you? One to a person."

When we crowded into the room I had been pushed against a side wall, and it was some time before I got anywhere near the distribution lines. That saved me from some bad mauling, for the first ones who got hold of a loaf of bread tried to turn back against the stream, and a terrible crush developed. Being near the door to an outside yard, I shouted to them to turn that way; many of them did, and I had time enough to notice that they must have found a way out, for they didn't come back. I also had time to realise that our crowd was no more than a few hundred strong, not the thousands I had imagined in the darkness.

Keeping close to the wall I edged forward. When I was near enough, I made it clear to the KPs behind their barrier that I wanted more than one loaf because I represented four prisoners, and supported my argument with the leg of a chair that I picked up from the barricade. They gave in, and I got two loaves and two containers of lard. Turning quickly, I sneaked back along the wall towards the blackout curtain, fearful lest other prisoners dispute my bounty. I found a short stone staircase that led up to a small, enclosed yard. Looking around, I saw an uncertain light coming from an opened doorway and made my way towards it, meanwhile wrapping the bread and the lard into the worn cotton apron that till then had been such a useless part of my prison uniform.

Once in the doorway, I shrank back, horrified by the scene that confronted me. It was a fairly small storeroom; along the walls and on the floor some thirty prisoners were fighting each other, clawing and pawing at the contents of many suitcases that had been piled up along the wall, but were now being ripped apart, their contents scattered, each new find causing new battles among the looters: I saw two politicals standing near me, not taking part in the mêlée, but staring at it with appalled fascination.

"What is this?" I asked, and they answered, "It's the guards' storeroom." I shrugged and prepared to make my way over the fighting bodies to the staircase at the other side of the room, for the whole thing disgusted me, but then I happened to glance up and just managed to hold back a shout of joy. There on a high shelf, apparently unnoticed by the fighting mob on the floor, was a row of glass jars full of preserved fruit, and what looked like wine bottles. In a flash I calculated that by climbing half-way up the staircase I could reach at least part of it. Putting a finger to my lips I turned to the two politicals beside me and pointed. Carefully and as stealthily as we could —for if these raging females became aware of our find, they would surely crush us to death in their onslaught—we picked our way to the staircase. My plan worked beautifully; with one foot on the staircase and the other on a lower shelf, I reached out and passed down to the others three jars of fruit and three bottles of wine. Then I stepped down and we hurried up the stairs unnoticed. At the top of the stairs we took one bottle and one jar each, and separated. Hugging my incredible treasures with both arms, I turned to the right in the dark corridor, guided mainly by the fact that a new wave of prisoners was surging past me towards the kitchens. My progress was extremely slow, for I was so fearful that a sudden encounter in the dark would break my precious glassware that I dared only move at a crawl, again sticking close to the wall. It might have taken me all night, but when I was about a third of the way along, the lights came on again and then I ran, dodging like a football player through the milling confusion of the corridors.

Joke and Nell had not been idle in the meantime. Once our floor had emptied, they had made their way to Fafa's cell and found her in front of it, clutching the stair rail for support, deserted by her cellmates. With Nell and Joke holding her up, she had managed the slow, painful shuffle to the corner cell and now she lay there, exhausted, on a pile of three mattresses. Her whole poor body was twisted with arthritis, and it was obvious that every movement was painful; yet her big dark eyes were blazing with light and her shrivelled little face radiated happiness. Once they had her installed, Nell and Joke had dragged four more mattresses to this cell; by piling up three of them and leaning the fourth against the wall on top of those, they had fashioned a kind of couch, covered with an extra blanket. They had also collected all our bowls and spoons and even some tin mugs. The door was safely propped open with some pieces of wood from a wall shelf that they had smashed for the purpose.

When I came panting up the stairs, they were ready for me. "Come into our palace!" said Nell, with one of the grand gestures that had earned her the odd nickname of "the Baron".

I kissed Fafa and proudly spread out my wares. The others goggled. "Baron," I said solemnly, "let's have a feast."

And a feast we had! From long training we kept one of the loaves of bread for the morning; the other one we broke up in four roughly equal pieces, smeared with lard. The jar, a two-quart one, proved to contain peaches and syrup. We were momentarily stumped by the cork in the wine bottle, but then Nell remembered that by happy coincidence she had been the guardian that week of the communal NN scissors, and with

C

those the cork was soon conquered. We divided up half of the wine, and it hit us so hard that we decided to keep the rest for another occasion. While we were happily enjoying this tasty and abundant meal, most of the other NNs drifted back to their cells and were staging their own celebrations. Many of them had returned with only the bread and lard, yet every cell had something extra. The group of Belgians opposite us had some raw rutabagas; next door somebody had snatched a pot of jam; and so on. All doors were open, the lights were now on in the cells too, and the wing rang with happy laughter. We had the whole wing to ourselves, for the Polish politicals never reappeared; they must have joined other Poles in another part of the prison.

After the feast, feeling momentarily sated for the first time in at least nine months, I felt another old craving, and said, "Now I wish I had a cigarette!"

"So do I," said Fafa and she added, "Look, you three ought to go out and see what the world is like on the outside. I'm all right now. Maybe you could even find me some tobacco." She was, of course, reading our thoughts. Although it was past midnight, we were all too excited to go to sleep, and we badly wanted to get out of this prison, if only for a little while. So we let Fafa convince us, and after hiding our embroideries, the wine, and the bread at the foot of her makeshift bed, we set out to reconnoitre. We were joined by a Belgian woman and her daughter, who had been cellmates of ours at one time. Excitedly, we clattered down the stairs in our wooden sandals. The main hallways were still bedlam— groups of prisoners surging in all directions, looking for friends or food, or simply giving vent to their emotions by dancing and shouting and rushing around madly. We joined hands in order not to lose each other, and moved like a human snake, Nell at the head, next to the two Belgians, then Joke and I at the tail. By asking over and over again, we found the right way to the exit, and, as we approached it, came upon more and more couples of Russian soldiers and German criminals rolling around

on the floor making love, oblivious of the feet that were stepping over them. Other Russians were roaming around with
happy anticipatory smiles on their faces. Yet there did not
seem to be any rape that first night; I saw no attacks and heard
no screams. The soldiers seemed to find as many willing partners as they needed, mostly among the better-fed criminal
prisoners.

Outside the heavy prison doors, which were thrown wide
open, we met an older Russian sergeant; at least, he seemed
much older than the young boys we had seen so far, but that
may have been simply because of his enormous handlebar
moustache. We encircled him and I asked, *"Papiroski? Papiroski?"* making extravagant smoking gestures. He smiled and
said, *"Da, da,"* and took Nell by the hand to lead us somewhere, supposedly towards cigarettes. Still in snake formation,
we crossed the dark street and entered the open door of a
house on the other side. As we filed into a short, narrow corridor, I suddenly came to my senses, let go of the hand of the
Belgian girl, turned round to Joke and said, "This is rather
dangerous. You'd better stay here and be sure to keep the door
open." Then I hurried after the others. The corridor, only a few
yards long, led into a lighted bedroom. To the right was a large
dressing-table topped by a huge mirror. In front of it stood
Nell and the two Belgian women, their mouths open, gaping at
their own reflections, completely unaware that on the double
bed behind them two couples were engaged in violent fornica-
tion. It was understandable enough; none of us had had a
chance to look in a mirror as long as we had been in prison,
and even though these three knew perfectly well how the
others around them looked, it still came as a great shock to
them to see their own pale, emaciated faces, their stringy,
lustreless hair, their shrunken bodies in the torn prison
clothing.

I looked around for our friend with the moustache, and just
at that moment he got up from where he had been crouched
down on the other side of the bed, rummaging in what must

have been his private stores. He gave me a big smile and came towards me with two big handfuls of cigars!

The whole situation was so ludicrous that I burst out laughing. This brought the other three out of their stupefaction. They took one look behind them and dashed past me like frightened rabbits. I paused long enough to accept the cigars and to indulge in a little pantomime with my Russian friend. Not knowing the word for "Thank you," I pointed at the cigars and nodded and smiled. He responded with a courteous gesture of invitation towards the bed. I shook my head with determination and he shrugged. I smiled at him again, he smiled back, and, still smiling, I retreated down the short corridor.

Outside, I found the others leaning against the wall, helpless with laughter, and we all stood there giggling, with me passing out cigars like a brand-new father. But when I saw Joke throwing her cigar away, I stooped to pick it up again and grew serious, saying, "Don't throw them away—we can exchange them for other things." Much as I was yearning for a smoke, I knew I couldn't tackle a big black cigar. So we divided them among us, stuffed them in our pockets, and continued our exploration. The streets were dark, except for the light of stars and moon, for all the houses were blacked out and the street lamps had probably been disconnected long ago. Yet throngs of people were out, and we knew they must all be either prisoners or liberators, for no German would have dared venture out on this night.

Holding hands again, we moved down the street we were in, not knowing where we were going or what we were looking for, just wanting to get a taste of this longed-for freedom. We had not gone far when we bumped into an American jeep parked in the middle of the street. Leaning against its hood, watching the confusion around them, were two American GIs. They probably were not much interested in this scene, which they must have witnessed several times before, not much concerned about who all these crazy prisoners were or what they wanted, but were just waiting till the crowd thinned out so that they could drive their jeep out of there and get back to where they could "hit the sack". But to us they were gods. They were the personification of the liberators we had dreamed of: smartly uniformed, strapping American soldiers, whose language we could understand, who could answer our myriad questions, who surely could tell us how to get out of this hell-hole.

We surrounded them and all started jabbering at once, and for a while didn't make any sense. But when we realised they were bored and didn't particularly want to bother with us, we made a great effort to get ourselves organised, to talk one at a time, to do anything that would please our gods. Faced with our sincerity and the urgency of our questions, they relented and became more friendly, and from them we learned for the first time that northern Holland was only just being liberated. This was a great disappointment. Our last news had been the parachute attack of 17 September 1944 on Arnhem, and we had assumed that shortly afterwards Holland, like Belgium and France, had been freed from the hated Nazi occupation.

The two Belgian women, having learned to their satisfaction that Belgium was free; not badly damaged, and actually thriving, moved on; but the three of us stayed and the two Americans, thawing even further, invited us into the jeep, where we sat in a huddle for about half an hour. They were extremely kind. Their answers about conditions in Holland were awkward and evasive, not because they didn't know (one of them let slip the information that V-2s had been launched from The Hague and that the town had been badly bombed) but because they wanted to spare us. They were delighted when I asked for cigarettes—it gave them a chance to switch the conversation from bad news to good—and, hunting around in the jeep and their pockets, they found nine cigarettes for us. They quite honestly excused themselves for keeping half a pack—they didn't know when they would get their next ration. I lit one on the spot and had to admit that it tasted like hay, to their great amusement.

Next they made us realise that we were inside the Russian lines and that they were only there by accident, as the spearhead of a patrol that had probed farther than they meant to. This information was hard to accept. "How are we going to get out of here and back to Holland?" we asked. "Who is going to help us if there are no American or British troops around?"

They didn't know the answer, but advised us to make our own way to the American lines; after that we would be taken care of. "We already have millions of you people," one of them added. It didn't sound very hopeful, but it was the best they could tell us. They also checked some of the rumours we had heard. Yes, Roosevelt had died. Yes, they had crossed the Rhine about two months ago. Well, yes, they too had heard that Hitler was dead, but they didn't know for sure. Anyway, the Nazis were capitulating everywhere, and the War was finished, as far as the big shooting was concerned. Yes, the Russians had surged over Poland and were now holding the country all around us. And so it went—questions and answers —and we could have kept at it all night, there was so much we didn't know. But they were plainly getting impatient to move. They gave us some souvenirs: a badge of their outfit (the 6th Armoured Division), a signed dollar (it was signed in the dark and I never managed to decipher the names), and a candy bar apiece. More because it was a promise we had made to ourselves than because they wanted it, we each kissed them in turn. They, as conquerors, had so obviously already had their pick of pretty girls everywhere, that they weren't in the least interested in three scarecrows like us. They had only been moved by pity and the goodness of their hearts, and maybe a little bit by the fact that we talked their language. And now they started their motor, the jeep moved off slowly through the crowd, and we stood in the middle of the street, sadly watching the retreat of our gods.

But nothing could keep us down that night; the restlessness born of long confinement kept pushing us along. So, a little wiser and a little richer with cigarettes and candy bars, we linked arms and set off down the street again, stopping now and then to inquire from other prisoners what was going on, shouting at intervals, "Hollanders—any Hollanders around here?" It wasn't till we had walked through two streets and had arrived at the entrance to the men's prison that we finally got an answer out of the crowd. A man's voice shouted, "Yes, I'm a Hollander. Where are you?"

It took five minutes of continuous shouting and searching before the voice became attached to a lanky young man who spread his arms wide, embraced all three of us in one big hug, and needed a few moments on our combined shoulders before he could trust his voice to speak normally. Even so, it had an odd high tune when he said, "Oh, my God, it's so good to speak Dutch again!"

The next few moments were a strange combination of shuffling and emotion. We were trying to get out of the throng and near a house wall on a pavement where we could draw up and talk quietly without being pushed; yet at the same time we were so eager to know more about each other that we would forget to move, and would ask questions to which we couldn't hear the answers because we were being buffeted from all sides. But at last we were established on the sill of a shuttered shop window, and Dries (for that was his name) told us his story. He had been caught trying to cross the Channel, had been condemned to death, had been put into the NN group and been moved from prison to prison whenever there was any remote chance of the Allies overrunning the town he happened to be in. So far his story was similar to ours. Also he had been brought to Waldheim at about the same time as we were. The difference was that he had been separated from other NNs and had spent the last three months in the company of two Norwegian smugglers who were simple fishermen by trade. These men, although kind, had not been smart enough to communicate with Dries in some language that would be understood by him but not by their fourth cellmate, a German criminal who was highly untrustworthy. Dries had been even lonelier than we during those last long months.

There was not much we could do for him, but at least we could relieve his loneliness. Almost in chorus we said, "Come and stay with us," and Dries came. The four of us started to make our way back. On the way, we told him our story and that we had Fafa to look after, and he assured us again that no matter how he had tried, he had not been able to contact any other Hollanders in the men's prison.

The crowds had thinned by now. There were still many prisoners around, and about an equal number of Russian soldiers, but we could walk abreast without trouble. Glancing up towards the sky, I realised that the moon must have gone down long ago and that the stars were paling in the first grey veil of dawn. When we climbed the steps to the women's prison, the church clocks rang out 4 a.m. We had been free for approximately five hours!

Fafa was dozing when we got back to our corner cell, but came wide awake when we introduced Dries. Having a man in our little family called for a new celebration, she decided, and when we discovered that all this time Dries had been carrying two loaves of bread and a half-pound can of lard under his arm, we merrily agreed. With the bread and lard, we drank the rest of the wine, and Fafa, Dries, and I had a cigarette. Nell and Joke declined; never having been confirmed smokers, they thought they might as well let the rest of us have that pleasure. This left us five cigarettes and eight crumpled cigars, which we stored away carefully with the rest of the bread and lard and the candy bars before we spread out the four mattresses that formed the couch. By this time we were reeling with fatigue; after Nell, being closest to the door, turned off the light switch on the outside, we sank into the sleep of the newly liberated.

Chapter Two

THE following days brought the full realisation that, although we were free, the prison was still our only home, and that no arrangements had been made by the conquering armies to take us back to our own homes some four hundred miles away. It was a cruel disappointment, especially to Nell, who had had visions of beflagged Red Cross buses that would drive us triumphantly through a defeated Germany, stopping every two hours or so for succulent meals to be served by humiliated Nazis.

Instead we were left to shift for ourselves.

Dries was already in civilian clothes, having searched out the prisoners' storeroom immediately after he had obtained his liberation bread. With several NNs we now went exploring, to see if any of our clothing had followed us and, if so, where it was stored. Up and down through the various wings and corridors we went, till eventually we found a storeroom on the top floor, which, amazingly enough, was still locked and therefore had not been looted. Breaking the door down didn't take long. Inside we found piles of prisoners' luggage: sacks, boxes, suitcases, all neatly labelled with prisoners' names or numbers. To us this was more evidence of the strange workings of the German mind: on the various hauls from one prison to another, the prisoners themselves had been so tightly packed into cattle-carts that some of them died; yet, somehow, room had been found to drag the worthless luggage along. And worthless it

41

was: Nell, Joke and I had had very little luggage, none of it valuable, stowed away in a pillow-case each. We found everything intact—in my case a pair of flannel slacks, a yellow sweater, some underwear, pyjamas, a pair of light sandals, and several tubes of vitamin pills. But some others were not so lucky. They could find their suitcases all right, but everything valuable that had been in them, such as fur coats, money, watches, and jewellery, was gone. Yet the luggage had followed us all the way!

We gratefully dumped our ragged, dirty prison clothes, and a mighty transformation came over the NN wing. We suddenly became people again instead of numbers, and so great was the change that I bumped into one of my former French cellmates without recognising her in her strange clothes and with her face so changed by a layer of cosmetics.

Then we ventured out into the town again, where every house was now decorated with a white flag and every shop window tightly shuttered. There were no Germans to be seen, only groups of ex-prisoners roaming everywhere in search of food, transportation, and a way out of the town. But it became clear very soon that there was no way out: the town was surrounded by the Red Army, there were sentries at every road and they had orders not to let anyone through, probably for the obvious reason that they could not distinguish between ex-prisoners and Germans. The soldiers came pouring in from all directions, and we marvelled at the variety of their vehicles. Some were in trucks, some in buses, and many, many more came in oxcarts and horsecarts, sometimes followed by strings of cattle. There seemed to be no rhyme or reason to their movements, but the appearance of disorder was deceptive, for their encampments around the town were well organised.

On the second day of our freedom Joke and I discovered the abandoned dairy plant. Gates and doors were open, and when we came upon it several other ex-prisoners were already inside, scouting for food. The cheese shelves were empty; so was a refrigeration room; but in another part of the plant we found five enormous, shiny vats with rungs on their sides for ladders. We climbed up quickly and were overjoyed to find the vats brimful of buttermilk. Soon there were two ex-prisoners at every vat, one foot hooked into a rung of the ladder, holding on to the rim and bending over to drink buttermilk till they had to come up for breath. Then they would come down and two others would clamber up and have their fill, and so on, by turns. On my second turn my foot slipped loose, and I would have tumbled in if Joke hadn't grabbed me. After the third turn we decided that we couldn't hold any more and that the lowered level of the buttermilk made this an extremely dangerous sport. So we found a big milk container, dipped it in the vat till it was filled up, lowered it to the floor without spilling too much, and proceeded to carry it back to the prison. However, we were so weak that even our combined forces weren't enough to lift the big container for more than a few paces, and our progress was extremely slow. After every few steps we would sit on the curb for a minute or so to regain strength, and by the time we had made it to the NN wing we were utterly exhausted.

But our success made the tremendous effort worthwhile. We fed Dries, Fafa and Nell till they felt the stuff was running out of their ears, had some more ourselves, distributed the rest among the other NNs, and went back for more, this time with Nell and Dries to help with the carrying. By now so many ex-prisoners had dipped into the vats that in most of them the level was too low to be reached, and we searched vainly for the method the workers at this plant had used to empty the vats. Finally, Dries and I knotted our leather belts together, and, by lowering the container on those, managed to get it about half full—enough to carry us through the evening and part of the next day. We still lived in the hope that something would happen soon, that we would not be required to live like outlaws for ever.

The next day we went back to the storeroom and discovered another behind it, this one was lined with closets chockfull of sheets, towels, napkins, and pillow-cases, many of them brand new and, as we well knew, never issued to prisoners. We helped ourselves to towels and sheets, and I also took six large napkins, thinking that I would take them home to my mother as a present. We then went through the small prison hospital, which was deserted. Weighing ourselves, we found that on the average we had lost a third of our weight. There was nothing in the hospital that could be of use to us, except a stretcher, which we took up to our cell in case we could transfer Fafa to better surroundings.

With that purpose in mind we went over to the hospital of the men's prison. This one we found still tenanted. It was much bigger than ours, with several bedrooms. A nurse and a doctor seemed to be in charge. Emaciated men, coughing and whining, occupied most of the beds, and we noticed there was one room with three free beds. We asked the harassed nurse if we could bring Fafa there. She shrugged and said yes, but she didn't know where food for these people was going to come from. She did, however, give us some aspirins for Fafa.

On our way back to take these to her, we noticed an old car standing in front of our prison. Hurrying over to see what was up, we were just in time to see a group of politicals bursting through the prison door. They were accompanied by a Russian soldier, and in their midst they held the fat doctor of the women's prison. Her head was completely shaved, tears were running down her face, and she was wailing loudly. We stood by as she was thrown down the steps, then bundled into the car with several ex-prisoners. Another soldier was at the wheel; he drove slowly off, with a throng of politicals hanging on to the car and running with it. It was all part of an unavoidable revenge. We already knew from Dries that in the men's prison several guards had been caught and hurled to their deaths through the stair-well. The doctor deserved whatever was coming to her, but we had no desire to be present when it happened. We heard later that she had been shot after a thorough beating.

We discussed with Fafa whether we should try to move her or not. The acquiescence of the nurse at the men's hospital had not meant exactly a warm welcome there, yet it might be a better place for her than this cell. The trouble was that Fafa was incapable of descending three steep flights of stairs and walking the short distance, while we were too weak to carry her, even on a stretcher. It also turned out that she did not want to be separated from us. She was thriving on our company and our friendship and, with a few full meals and the psychological lift of being free, she was already feeling much better. "Just leave me here for a few more days. Maybe I'll be able to walk then," she said.

On the fourth day the Russians suddenly showed that they were aware of our existence, and showed it in the nicest imaginable way. By this time the ex-prisoners were trying to organise themselves, and a meeting of the various groups and wings had been called in the sitting-room of the head of the prison, which faced a courtyard and the rear entrance. As the news of this meeting was haphazardly word-of-mouth, only about half of all the ex-prisoners were represented, but the NNs had heard about it and sent me down. The meeting was highly inconclusive. Some politicals, whom I suspected of being Communists, tried hard to pass official resolutions, but the other two dozen or so present were not interested in verbal fireworks. All we wanted was regular food and a chance to go home. The upshot was that one of the Czech politicals, who could talk to the Russians, was delegated to go and find whoever was in charge and impress our wishes upon him.

Just as the meeting broke up, around noon, an enormous Russian truck squeezed through the rear entrance and into the courtyard. It was loaded with what looked like rows of oil-drums and several gay Russian soldiers who beckoned us over. As we crowded around, the oil-drums were swung down. They contained big hunks of steaming boiled pork. Almost before I knew it, a large wooden tray was hung around my shoulders by a leather strap, and one of the soldiers was grabbing the

chunks of meat with both hands and loading them onto my
tray. When it was full, I staggered off in the direction of our
quarters. Even while I was climbing the stairs, I realised how
fat the meat was and what havoc this would play with our
unaccustomed stomachs; yet I could hardly wait to get my
hands on it. I served the NNs first, putting it in the bowls of
those who weren't present and warning the others, "Eat it
slowly and not all of it at one time; keep some for tomorrow."
I might as well have talked to the walls. There was still plenty
left, so I went down one floor and distributed the rest among
the politicals there, none of whom I had seen at the meeting.
Then it was my turn. I found myself grabbing the slippery
meat with both hands, eating big mouthfuls at once, barely
chewing till I got to the last few bites, my own admonitions
completely forgotten.

I took the tray back to where the Russians were now chatting
and smoking around the truck, and, as one of them spoke a
few words of German, I learned from him the Russian for
"thank you" (*spasibo*) and for "food" (*peshcha*).

Then I joined my friends again for another of our exploring
trips, this time to the town hall. This was an old Gothic-style
building on the main square; it had already been thoroughly
ransacked, but was still a good place to look for such treasures
as pencils and paper. Wandering through the various offices
with their torn and trampled portraits of Hitler, we found
plenty of both in desk drawers and closets, and Dries, poking
through a mountain of overthrown files, came upon other
riches: two maps, one of the whole of Germany, one of the
province of Saxony, where we were. This enabled us for the
first time to pinpoint our own position, for, although we knew
the name of the town we were in, we had never heard of it
before we arrived there and knew only vaguely that it was situated somewhere near Czechoslovakia. Now we found that we
were roughly thirty miles west of Dresden, thirty miles north
of the Czechoslovakian border, twenty-five miles from Altenburg, beyond which the American lines were supposed to

start, and about four hundred miles from home. Although at the moment this knowledge was only of theoretical use to us, at least it gave us a feeling of getting our feet on the ground.

In the next office we entered, a young Russian private was struggling with a typewriter on a desk near a window. He had a piece of paper in it at an odd angle and was pecking at the keys, rather apprehensively, with one finger. Being used to his own Russian characters, he was manifestly disturbed by the strange alphabet that appeared on his paper. Finally, he hit a lot of keys at once, and seeing that it still didn't produce any Russian, he picked up the typewriter and heaved it through the closed window, causing a great noise of breaking glass, which we hoped would warn the passers-by below. He looked around and, seeing us, gave us a big grin and reached for a crumpled ball of red cloth that had been lying at his feet. Spreading it out with his arms wide, he showed us that it was a soiled Nazi flag; then, taking a careful hold at a corner, he tore it diagonally across, right through the swastika. We applauded. He immediately gathered the pieces together and, with his strong hands, tore them again in the other direction. Stepping up to him, we shook his hand, clapped him on the shoulder, and laughed happily with him as the torn flag followed the typewriter through the window.

Our next move was to check up on the sentries guarding the bridge that led to the road to the west. They were still there, and as firm as ever. Beyond the bridge we could see the road going slightly uphill till it was lost in the trees that covered the hill on the horizon. The stretch we could see was badly pockmarked by shell-holes. On the left, beyond the bridge, was the old railway station, now a busy camp of the Red Army. There were no trains in sight, and not a chance of sneaking by unseen. On the right the road was bordered by flat fields that would give no cover, even provided we had the strength to try a cross-country trek, which we certainly had not. While we stood there, gazing rather forlornly in the direction we wanted to go, I suddenly felt a savage twist of pain in my insides; the boiled pork had begun its work! At the double, we scurried back to our quarters, only just in time before the first serious cramps attacked us.

There were no flushing toilets in our prison, and we had set up toilet buckets in three of the empty cells formerly occupied by the Poles. This arrangement had been adequate to give some much-desired privacy to all of the NNs. Now, suddenly, it was far from sufficient. Fafa needed the cell next door, to which she could shuffle on her own. Dries needed a place where women in dire need would not burst in upon him, and the rest of us just needed plenty of buckets. We accordingly set up a whole row in the washroom, and the entire prison spent a very convulsive night, full of groanings and anguished runs for the nearest unoccupied bucket.

The morning found us thoroughly purged, and weak as new-born kittens. We slept late to make up for the exhausting night, and when a political from the lower floor came running up to pass the word that food was being distributed at the men's prison, we were only mildly interested. Yet our own supplies were down to one hard crust of bread, and we knew that pretty soon we would be back to normal and hungry again. So we slowly got up.

Just as we came filing out of the prison door, we saw a sight that brought us fully alive. A big wagon drawn by two horses came lumbering up the street toward us, chock-full of men and women ex-prisoners standing behind the driver or sitting on suitcases farther back. Next to the driver sat a tall blond young man waving a big, handmade Czech flag. I recognised some of the women in the wagon as Czech politicals and waved and shouted to them in German, "Where are you going?" and the whole wagonful shouted back, "We're going home! Hurrah, we're going home!"

We stood and waved at them till they disappeared behind the bend. "Well," said Dries, "obviously the Czechs are nearest to their homes, but if they are allowed to go, maybe it'll be our turn soon."

"Hey," exclaimed Joke, "look around you! All the houses have red flags!"

And so they had. Instead of the sheets and towels that had served as white flags on the buildings during the first four days, big red flags were now hanging from every flag pole and from many window sills as well. Going up to one of them that hung quite low, I could see clearly the outline of the swastika that had been removed. "The sons of bitches," I said, and we all laughed. Then from my pocket I drew the sharp knife I had picked up during one of my explorations, and cut off a long strip of red cloth.

"What do you want that for?" asked Nell, in a tone which plainly indicated that touching a Nazi flag, even with the swastika torn off, should be beneath my dignity.

"Did you see that those Czechs had made a flag?" I said. "We had better make ourselves flags too, so everybody can see that we are Hollanders. This will do fine for the red. We can sew them on our clothes, just little ones, but big enough for people to see."

They all agreed to this idea, and we decided to look out for some blue cloth, knowing that we already had a plentiful source of white in the prison sheets. Meanwhile we had arrived at the men's prison and turned through the big portal into a wide central courtyard. On our left were the kitchens; in front of them long trestle tables had been set up, around which clusters of ex-prisoners, men and women, were milling about. Joining them, we saw that several men in grey overalls were indeed distributing food—whole loaves of bread and small cans of ersatz jam. We each got our share, then we held Nell's while she went around for an extra share for Fafa. This strategem worked so well that Dries went around an extra time too. He returned with the news that there would be a daily distribution and that we needn't bother to hoard the food. We discovered that the turmoil in our insides had subsided, so we sat down in the sun on some stone steps and had a quiet meal. While we were still eating, a small file of women in prison garb

D

came out of one of the kitchen doors and, under the direction of another man in grey, started to peel potatoes around a big pail. We were watching them with interest and commenting that the Russians were really getting things in hand if they already had picked up some Nazi prisoners of their own, when Nell suddenly exclaimed, "They are our guards!"

We rushed over for a good look. Sure enough, the women were four of our former guards, now decked out in prison clothes identical with those we had worn for so long, except that theirs looked fresh and new. It was a great moment. We stood around them, looking them over and discussing them in Dutch, which they could not understand, but which they knew very well could not mean a word of good about them. Every time we pointed at them, they cringed, "Look, Zip," said Joke excitedly, "there's the 'gorilla', the one you wanted so much to kill!"

I stared fixedly at the woman, at those coarse features and that cruel mouth I had hated from the bottom of my soul. Yes, it was true, many times I had vowed to kill her if I could lay hands on her; yet now I found that, even had I known how to go about it in a sunny courtyard full of people, I was incapable of killing in cold blood. It was not the presence of the grey-clad man that held me back—he took no notice of us whatsoever—nor the fact that my friends were standing around me. I could feel them waiting tensely, willing to do whatever I decided was to be done. It wasn't even the absence of any suitable weapon, for in a flash of a second I considered whether I would try for a direct knock-out on the chin, or lift up the pail and bring it down on her head, or rely on the help of my friends to strangle her. I could not do it, because something in my background, in the many imponderables that conspire to make a person act or not act at any given moment, made me realise quite clearly that by doing it I would irretrievably bring myself down to the level of those whom I despised so much.

Once this was clear to me, however, I was not beyond a little sadism. The woman had become extremely uneasy under my sustained stare and was now babbling incoherently about how good she had always been and how she had to obey orders. She could not flee, for the man in grey was almost directly behind her. So I took one menacing step forward and thoroughly enjoyed seeing how she wobbled at the knees and threw up her hands to her face. Then I spat contemptuously at her feet and turned away, with the others following me.

We now set out on a tour of the men's prison, of which apparently only the kitchen wing was in official use by the men in the grey overalls. We speculated that they must be local Communists, for they spoke perfect German although they were obviously working for the Russians. We wondered where they had been hiding all this time, but didn't break our heads over it. We had other worries, such as where to get a pair of shoes for me. My sandals had been in none too good shape when we were transferred to Germany, and if some day we had to make our own way to the American lines, as our GI friends had said, I would need something sturdier. Dries said he thought there had been a cobblers' workshop in the prison, although he had never actually seen it, so we set out to look for it and eventually found it at the end of a long row of communal cells. It was an absolute shambles. Benches and tools had been overthrown and the floor was littered knee-deep with shoes of every size and description—hundreds and hundreds of shoes, but none of them paired! We spent hours wading through the pile and crawling over it before Dries picked up a pair of loafers and I found a pair of strong, well-soled man's shoes with iron guards on the heels. They were heavy, and one size too big for me, but it was the best we could do. We never found anything that remotely fitted Joke. Nell, who had left us to take Fafa her food, was satisfied with her own.

Roaming farther through the maze of corridors and cell blocks, we met a group of young Frenchmen, who told us that another wagonload of Czechs had just left and that a big group of Poles had been allowed to go east on foot. Things were loosening up! One of the Frenchmen was munching a piece of hard cheese and I asked him where he had found it. He grinned and answered, "Organised."

The verb "to organise" had been widely in use in the prisons and camps and simply meant to acquire what one needed by stealing, bamboozling, or any other means at one's disposal. Similar to it, in those first days of freedom, was another verb: "to liberate". This meant to take anything useful one happened to find, without inquiring into rightful ownership. The distinction was slight, yet to us it marked the transition from a world where even the strictly necessary was mostly lacking, to a world where one could lay claim to such luxury as an extra pair of shoes.

The Frenchman proved very obliging. "Would you like some cheese?" he asked, and then took us along to a communal cell with twelve bunks, many of them loaded with all kinds of clothes, shoes, and packages. Unrolling a blanket from his own bunk, he uncovered about three-quarters of a five-pound wheel of cheese and cut off a generous hunk for us. We gave him two of our cigars, which pleased him greatly. Then we joined Nell and Fafa for our evening meal and the usual leisurely chat before nightfall.

The prison was noticeably emptier. In addition to the criminals freed by the Germans before the liberation, those who had been kept on the kitchen and household details had now disappeared, supposedly to homes in the neighbourhood. Most of the Poles and Czechs had left that day, and the rest were preparing to take off the next morning. The wing of communal cells that had belonged to the second category (what we used to call the prostitute class) of prisoners, was almost deserted, and we assumed that most of the inmates were now plying their trade for the Red Army. So the prison was left pretty much in the hands of politicals from the Western countries, including our little band of NNs. Everybody was feeling hopeful that night, and we sang many of our old songs. One cell would start and another would pick up the song, then another, until our whole wing was ringing with "Show Me the

Way to Go Home", "I've Got Sixpence", "Madelon", and the
many other songs of which we had kept the tunes but changed
the words. Joke and Nell were excellent harmonisers, and Dries
was so touched by our singing that he showed us his treasure:
a square of cotton on which he had embroidered a lighthouse,
marked with his mother's address, which sent a powerful beam
in the direction of a small figure behind bars, which represented Dries himelf. We showed him ours in turn and a new
and powerful bond established itself—the kind of bond that
comes from discussing embroidery techniques with a merchant seaman.

Another ex-prisoners' meeting was scheduled for the next
afternoon, but it never took place. When we rounded the corner towards the men's prison a little before noon, on our way
to the food distribution, we saw a sight that made our hearts
leap: a convoy of six big American trucks! The front ones were
swarming with ex-prisoners. We broke into a run and accosted
the US major who was standing at the tailboard of the last
truck, directing all comers. "Hurry up," he said to us, "I'll try
to take out as many of you as I can, but I can't stand here all
day. We're not even supposed to be here."

But things weren't so easy. "Can you take a sick woman
who's crippled with arthritis?" we asked.

He looked at us, swallowed a few curses, and said, "Impossible. The roads are shot to hell. Besides, they'll be packed in
these trucks like sardines. There are many more of you than I
thought. Can she stand?"

We shook our heads. "No, and you'd have to help us carry
her. She's on a top floor."

"Sorry," he said, "can't help you then." He turned to the
third truck and motioned to the driver that he could start letting people on. The first two trucks were already jammed tight.
Then he said to us, "If you're not coming, you'd better warn
the other women. Tell them to hurry, we've got to get out of
here fast."

"But Dries can go," said Joke suddenly.

"If you aren't going, I'm not either," said Dries gruffly, and
with that we started running back to the women's prison, shouting the news to all we met on the way. In almost no time a
general exodus to the trucks was under way. We rushed up to
the NN wing to warn the others and to tell Fafa not to worry.
When we thought all of them had left, I made a quick check of
the cells and in the last one I found the elderly Belgian woman
of the pink-threaded girdle, sound asleep. I shook her roughly,
gathered up her belongings, got her to her feet and dragged
her with me down the stairs, explaining all the way. Hand in
hand we ran along the street, both of us stumbling, I in my
wide shoes, which I had proudly put on that day, she from
general weakness.

We made it just in time, for the trucks were ready to pull
out. There seemed to be no room left among the closely packed,
standing men and women on the last truck, but helpful hands
reached out and pulled the little Belgian woman aboard.
"*Merci, merci,*" she cried to me, tears running down her face.
"Come and see me." She even added an address, but I couldn't
hear it in the roar of the truck starting up. Suddenly I saw,
backed up against the cab of the truck, Lottie, the young
Belgian girl who had been so surprised at her own image in
the mirror, and her mother, and Laure, my old cellmate.

I started to run along the now slowly moving truck, yelling
as loudly as I could, "Tell the Red Cross Fafa is here!" I kept
repeating it, praying they would hear me and finally Lottie did.
"*Oui, oui,*" she yelled back, "Red Cross—Fafa. Good-bye, Zip!"

Her answer came in the nick of time, for I was exhausted and
we had now reached the town square, where the trucks could pick
up speed. Panting, I sat down on the curb and waved at the
trucks till the last one had turned the corner in the direction
of the bridge. Then I walked slowly back the way I had come.
I was feeling lonely and defeated and not even sure that we
had made the right decision. Naturally, we couldn't have left
Fafa behind. Well, then maybe half of us should have gone to
make sure that the Red Cross got the right information and got

it fast. Joke should have gone; she was the youngest. But it was almost axiomatic for Nell, and Joke, and me to stick together; we had done it for so long and through so many hardships. It would have been impossible to persuade Joke to leave. Well, why did Dries stay? I had just reached this point in my thoughts when I saw Dries coming towards me from the portal of the men's prison. He had obviously been looking for me and waved cheerily.

"You should have gone with them," I said accusingly as he came up to me.

He laughed. "You girls are all the same," he answered lightly. "I've just been getting hell from the others. How do you think you'd make out with four girls among all these Russkis if you didn't have a man with you?"

So that was it. This emaciated fellow, whose muscles had been wasted away by more than a year of confinement, whose clothes were floating around his thin frame, whose face was still drawn from hunger, was going to be our protector! Yet his remark touched me deeply, and I reflected that protection didn't consist of muscles alone. I slipped my arm through his and said, "We'd better go and see if they'll give us some food." Together we turned into the courtyard of the men's prison. The trestle tables were still there; sitting on them, all by himself in the empty courtyard, was the stocky man in grey who had been there the day before. He looked friendly enough, with his apple cheeks, his crew-cut of grey hair, and his light blue eyes behind rimless glasses. We asked him if there would still be food for us, now that most of the prisoners had left.

"They haven't all gone," he said. "There wasn't enough room on the trucks. One or two groups stayed behind somewhere over there." He indicated the other side of the courtyard. "Besides, there must be others who were out in the town somewhere and never knew about the trucks. Sure, I'll have some food for you here." He went into the kitchen and returned a little later with two loaves of bread and a small can of lard under one arm, and a bowl of soup and two spoons in his other hand. "Go ahead and eat," he said, putting the bowl in front of us. Since we hadn't eaten anything hot since the boiled pork, we fell to with alacrity. "How come you didn't leave on the trucks?" he asked.

Between spoonfuls of good pea soup, we told him, and Dries handed over two cigars, for this friendship seemed worth cultivating. He lit one right away and, puffing on it thoughtfully, said, "You'd better get your sick friend out of the women's prison, for that has to be cleared tomorrow. It's going to be used again."

This was a new problem. "How?" we asked. "We can't carry her."

"I don't know," he said. "I'm just telling you."

Wondering how this man knew so much, I asked him, "Who are you?" But he laughed and, throwing out his arms in an all-inclusive gesture, only answered, "I'm the cook here."

After that we were careful never to ask him any questions about himself or about the origin of his knowledge; not only were we dependent on him for food, but he was a trustworthy source of news, and in the absence of radio, newspapers, or even a reliable grapevine, we sorely needed one. We chatted some more with him and heard that a military government had been established in the town and that the shops had been ordered to open the next day, so life would be returning more or less to normal. He also advised us to move into the men's prison if we thought we had to stay longer, for he estimated that would not be in use for another week. Finally he brought out a gallon pail of soup for us to take to the others and with that we left, heavy of heart, wondering how we would move Fafa, and how we would ever get home ourselves.

In spite of the soup, that last evening in the now practically deserted prison was a dismal one; none of us slept much as we lay in the darkness, turning our problems over in our minds.

Chapter Three

We had worried too soon! The following morning, when we went out to try to find help for the dangerous job of carrying Fafa downstairs, the first people we met were two soldiers in Dutch uniform. Before we had quite got over our surprise at so incongruous a sight as a Dutch uniform, the whole street was swarming with them. We quickly made ourselves known, and for a while we held court on the curb in front of the prison, surrounded by a happy, laughing crowd of young soldiers of Her Majesty Queen Wilhelmina. All of them had spent the five long war years in a prisoner-of-war camp near Dresden, to the east of us. The Russians, after keeping them there for five days, had set them free two days ago, telling them that they should go west to the American lines and that their uniforms would serve as passes. They all looked healthy and well fed; they told us that the food in their camp had been monotonous but sufficient and that they also had received Red Cross packages and even, occasionally, packages from their families. They had had to work, but the hours had been easy and none of the work too heavy. Evidently it had been much better to be a prisoner of the German Army than of the Gestapo!

Even so, five years is a terribly long time in anybody's life, and these boys were eager to be on their way. The crowd around us dwindled rapidly, and before they all disappeared, we quickly stated our problem and asked their help. They did not hesitate. Four of them stepped forward and said, "Sure, where is she?"

We led them into the prison; as their heavy boots clanged on the iron stairs, we shouted up to Fafa, "Don't worry, Fafa, the Dutch Army is going to move you!"

With infinite tenderness these four strangers wrapped Fafa in a blanket, placed her on the stretcher, and lifted it with careful ease. Fafa was too overcome to speak, and I myself felt tears stinging my eyes as the triumphant procession went down the stairs, out of the prison, and through the streets to the men's hospital.

Once we had her safely bedded down there, the soldiers asked cheerfully, "Anything else you want done before we leave?"

Joke said timidly, "Would you mind very much going through the prison with us, to see if there are any other sick that are left behind? You see, the Russians are going to use the prison, and if there are any more left, they might never get out."

Joke had a pretty, round face, set in a halo of frizzly blond hair, and she looked even younger than her scant twenty years. She was hard to resist under any circumstances, but when she asked for a favour in her particular brand of childishness and gravity, nobody could refuse her. Although they must have been in a tearing hurry to be off, the soldiers courteously consented and together we made the rounds of the whole prison. As Joke had feared, there were two more badly-ill women in the downstairs communal cells. Both were obviously tubercular and in high fever. The stretcher came into use again; our patient soldiers carried those two to the hospital also, where the gruff doctor gave them an injection against the fever and provided another stretcher so that we could leave the women outside, where the fresh air would do them more good than the stale hospital smell inside.

Now at last we could wish our soldier friends *bon voyage.* We accompanied them to the bridge to the west and, after grateful farewells, watched how the Russian sentry motioned them through on sight.

"Boy," sighed Dries, "how I wish I had a uniform!" We all did, but we smiled bravely at each other and returned to the women's prison to gather up our own possessions. As our cook friend had advised, we transferred to the men's prison. After some careful scouting, we found a corner cell that had manifestly belonged to some privileged criminals; it had two big windows looking over the courtyard, four wooden bunks, and a small wood-stove. We were heartily sick of living in cells and behind barred windows, but this was an improvement over our arrangements in the NN wing.

In another talk with the cook, who again treated us to bread and soup, we found out that there was a civilian hospital on the eastern outskirts of the town. He said he didn't think that road was closed any more, adding, "It's the way the Poles went." He had been right about the shops opening this day and we were quite willing to trust his advice that we inquire at the civilian hospital the next day whether they could take our patients. After all, we would have to leave Fafa some day, for her recovery might take months, and, as it was now practically certain that we would have to make the trek to the American lines on foot, it was impossible to take her with us. The problem, therefore, was to find her a safe place where she would have some medical care till the Red Cross came after her with an ambulance. A civilian hospital would certainly be better than the make-shift prison hospital, which the Russians might take over any day.

We were still discussing all this with the cook when we heard loud noises and cheers coming from the street. We went to the portal and again found the street full of soldiers, this time in French uniform. Talking to a few of them, we soon discovered that, like the Dutchmen in the morning, they had been released from a POW camp and been told to go west. But there the similarity ended. Compared with the gay exuberance of this crowd, the happy, laughing boys of the morning had been as solemn as undertakers. And, whereas the Dutch had taken great care of their uniforms while wearing their German-issued work clothes to shreds (as one of them had told us), and had lovingly shined their buttons in expectation of the trip home, the French looked like the tatterdemalion army of some beggar king. Each of them had at least one piece of the French uniform, but it was hard to find one among them who had a complete uniform in good shape. There were fatigue trousers, peasant smocks, woollen shirts in all colours, and at least two Russian tunics, which the wearers had evidently managed to swap against their own. There were army berets, but as many black civilian berets, and a host of miscellaneous headgear.

But the biggest difference was in the luggage. The Dutch had come through with at most a knotted kerchief carried in one hand or on a stick over the shoulder. The four who had helped us had nothing except the uniforms on their backs. But the French are great organisers and improvisers, and obviously hadn't lost their art during the long years of imprisonment. They were loaded down with assortments of luggage ranging from gunny sacks to shiny suitcases, and several groups of them were prodding along small donkeys loaded with wicker hampers, bulging pillow-cases, and even demijohns. They had not lost their sense of humour either. While we were talking to one of them, another with a huge bag on his shoulder and a suitcase in his hand stopped to say, "You think I'll ever get this stuff home to France? Never, my dears, never! It will crush me to death." With that he shifted his load, laughed loudly, and continued on his way.

Others passed by, pulling small carts behind them, mostly consisting of crates fixed to a pair of small wheels. Right in front of us, the rope attached to one of these carts broke, and one end of it got tangled in the wheel. Impatiently, the soldier who had been pulling it kicked the cart aside, shouldered his pack, and moved on. Dries promptly pounced on the little wagon and drew it into the safety of the portal, saying over his shoulder to us, "We'll need something like this."

When the last of this gay and noisy army had passed by, we paid a visit to Fafa. She was resting fairly comfortably and had

been fed and given aspirin. We regaled her with a description
of the French antics we had just witnessed; then we discussed
a further move to the civilian hospital. Courageous as she was,
she fully agreed, and urged us to start on our way home as
soon as possible. "You've done enough for me already," she
said, "and it'll take longer than I thought before I can walk
again. You can't stay here indefinitely. The Russians wouldn't
even let you."

That night, while a small pail of soup was heating on the
wood-stove, which we had stoked up with odds and ends of
wreckage that could be gathered all around the prison, Dries
got out his maps and said, "Look, I have a plan. It seems that
the Russkis have taken off all the sentries except on the road
to the west. Maybe they'll take that one off, too, and then we'll
just follow the trucks and the soldiers. But if they don't, then
why don't we go north? According to this map, it's about thirty
miles to this town Riesa. That's on the Elbe river. Now the
Elbe goes to Hamburg and you heard from the Americans that
Hamburg is in British hands. I bet we can find a rowboat or a
couple of canoes in Riesa, and then all we'll have to do is drift
downstream to Hamburg. There the British will help us, and
anyway Hamburg is a lot closer home than this godforsaken
place."

It sounded simple and attractive. We all pored over the
maps. The distance to Riesa was about the same as that to
Altenburg, where, rumour had it, the American lines began.
"Are you sure there's no sentry on the road north?" Nell asked.

"No, I'm not," confessed Dries, "but they're off south and
east, so why not north also? That leads into their own territory
too, as far as I understand. Anyway, that's easy to check."

"We'll need some food," I said, "and something to carry our
stuff in."

"That's why I took that little wagon the French soldier threw
aside," said Dries triumphantly.

"Matter of fact," mused Joke, "I like this plan better than
going straight west. Remember how the Americans said they

already had millions like us? And then there's the people they
picked up here, and all those soldiers. If we'll have to travel
from place to place standing up in trucks, I'd much rather sit
in a boat and go down the river on our own till we're close to
home."

"Joke, you're a girl after my own heart," said Dries, throwing
his arms around her.

Indeed, Dries's plan had a special appeal to all of us. During
all the time of our imprisonment only one subject had been
taboo in all our cell talk; that was water sports, sailing and
swimming included. We had discovered early that the image
of a sailboat on a sunny lake, of a swimmer poised to dive, of a
canoe skimming lightly over the water, represented to all
three of us the epitome of freedom, and that we just couldn't
stand it when spoken words brought to a sudden pitch the constant yearning of our hearts. But now we were free, and here
was Dries, the seaman, holding before us the enchanting prospect of a boat trip down a wide river. No wonder we were all
smiling when, after long and excited discussion of this new
possibility, we climbed into our bunks.

We spent the next days in thorough preparation. First of all
we presented ourselves at the civilian hospital and lost half the
day finding somebody in authority whom we could talk to
about our three sick people. The German staff didn't dare turn
us down, as they undoubtedly would have under other circumstances, but merely kept sending us from pillar to post in the
hope that we would give up. We persisted, however, and finally
found an elderly doctor who was both willing to listen to us
and able to do something about it. He left us, to check up on
the number of beds available, and returned with the welcome
news that we could bring our patients in two days. Practical as
ever, Nell asked him to make sure that the admission staff knew
about it, and also requested some help in the transportation of
our sick. He promised this, too.

All during the interview, the doctor never moved a muscle in
his face. He behaved rather like one of those old-fashioned

Prussian officers whom we had read about or seen in the movies, but only rarely spotted among the occupation troops —extremely correct, but icy as the North Pole. His attitude made it quite clear that he still considered us enemies, but that he knew his duties, both towards enemy sick and as an officer of a vanquished army. This suited us very well. We still hated all Germans, and needed no excuse for it. We even loathed to speak the language, although we often had to because it was the only lingua franca between us and the Slavic peoples (such as Poles, Czechs, and Russians), and because it was imperative whenever we had to deal with the Germans around us. But an attitude such as the doctor's was easier on us than even the friendliness of the ambiguous cook. The lines were clearly drawn, and whenever communication was necessary each side was allowed to keep its own dignity.

The contrast was therefore all the greater when we met our next German character. Under the portal of the men's prison was a door that led to what had been the office of the prison director. It had been thoroughly sacked and up till now had remained untenanted. But when we returned from the hospital we found a tall man in flashy clothes lounging in the doorway. He came right up to us with outstretched hand—which all four of us ignored—and explained that he was the new director of the prison, that he had heard we were temporarily staying there, that we were quite welcome and was there anything we needed?

"Yes," said Dries bluntly, "cigarettes."

"Of course, of course," said the man, and ducked into the office.

I shot Dries an admiring glance. All of us had instantly and instinctively recognised the fellow as the kind of operator that used to run black markets during the War, and our first reaction was to have nothing to do with him. Yet Dries had taken the right track: if the man was who he said he was, we would have to put up with him, and we might as well get something out of it.

He popped out of his doorway with a packet of cigarettes for each of us and two big boxes of kitchen matches. Recognising the brand of cigarettes as the kind the Gestapo used to smoke, I trusted the man even less, but they were better than nothing, and the matches were a godsend, so we thanked him politely, keeping our distance.

A little later we said to the cook, "So you have a new director?"

"Yeah," he said. "Want some more soup?"

Plainly, he didn't like the fellow either. Dries decided to play it bold and asked, "When we decide to hit the road, could you give us some supplies?"

The cook surveyed us critically from under his eyebrows. "Sure I could," he said slowly, "sure I could. But where do you think you're going?"

"Just west," said Dries airily, "they let all the soldiers through, didn't they? Why shouldn't they let us through?"

"That's what the Frenchies are planning," chuckled the cook, "but I don't think any of you will make it. Why don't you wait a little longer? There's a camp being made ready for you people near Dresden."

"Dresden!" squealed Nell, "but that's east of here!"

"So what?" he rejoined, "you can get home just as well that way. Over Odessa."

We tried to press him further, but he clammed up, and we retreated to our corner cell to mull over this latest bit of disconcerting news. From our geography books and from the more recent war news, we knew that Odessa was a Ukranian port on the Black Sea. We were not sure about the distance from Waldheim to Odessa, but were quite convinced that it was appreciably longer than the four hundred-odd miles from Waldheim to Holland. And even if we reached Odessa without mishap—which was unlikely through a countryside that until recently had been occupied and ravaged by the German armies —getting home would still mean a voyage through the Mediteranean and a long over-land trip through France and Belgium. We decided that it would be the slowest and most ridiculous way to travel and that we would have no part of it.

After a brief visit to Fafa, we walked over to the bridge to check on the sentry. He was still there, and so was the encampment at the railway station. We returned to the town square and took a winding street that led north from it. At the bottom of a steep hill, the street changed abruptly into a gravel road that climbed up the hill and out of sight. There were no sentries to be seen. So far, so good.

In the meantime, the town had taken on an air of near-normalcy. Not only were the shops open, but the inhabitants had ventured out of the houses where they had been hiding like moles for almost a week, and were now hurrying busily along the streets. The town hall had been taken over by the Russian *Kommandant*, and we saw several people lugging shot-guns and rifles to the new *Kommandatura*. Evidently there had been an order to turn in all weapons, and the Germans, obedient as ever, were bringing them by the armful.

Ambling along, taking it all in, we were suddenly startled by Nell, who shouted, "Blue!" and set off after a young man in blue trousers who had come into view a hundred yards ahead of us. Just as she got to him, the young man opened a door and disappeared. Nell disappeared with him. The rest of us waited expectantly in front of the doorway, ready to barge in if we heard cries for help, but after five minutes Nell emerged, triumphantly holding a long strip of blue cloth. She never would tell us whether she had forcibly taken the man's trousers off or whether, thus threatened, he had hurriedly found some other blue cloth in his household. But that night, around our wood-stove, the three of us girls sewed together half a dozen Dutch flags, while Dries tinkered with the little wagon the Frenchman had left behind. We proudly attached the flags to our sweaters, Nell's extra blouse, and Dries's jacket. As there was some cloth left, we made some smaller flags for the rucksacks we hoped to obtain.

All this time Dries had been swearing copiously at his work;

E

when we took a closer look at what he was doing, we saw that the cart consisted of a crate mounted on baby-buggy wheels. Joke immediately christened it "The Pram". Dries had been reinforcing the crate with pieces of board and wire he had collected, but without proper tools he was unable to fix the left wheel, which wobbled a little. We tested the contraption by loading all our blankets and some firewood on it and wheeling it down the corridor. It held, so we went to sleep gratified.

The next day we tried to sound out the two groups of French ex-prisoners who were still staying at the prison, about what they were going to do next. Up to then we had seen them around regularly, but had had little contact with them. We had nothing against them, but simply had enough problems of our own and did not want to get involved in any others. They obviously felt the same way and were very cagy about their plans. This we fully understood; we did not want to divulge ours, either. We noticed, however, that both groups had apparently persuaded one of the French soldiers to stay with them, and from the profusion of clothing and material lying around their communal cells, we guessed that they were in the process of collecting some semblance of uniforms so that they could pass as POWs. To us, that meant they planned to go directly west, and we wished them good luck.

One fellow was sitting cross-legged on his bunk, sewing industriously, surrounded by several pieces of green canvas. I fingered one of them and asked him where he had found it. "The storeroom over there is full of it," he answered, indicating the direction with his chin. We wandered off that way and indeed found a storeroom where scores of heavy rolls of canvas had been thrown around in a mountainous jumble. The temptation to take quantities of it was great, for it was high-quality stuff that would serve many purposes, but, remembering the French soldier who feared he would be crushed to death by his luggage before he got home, we reasonably cut off only as much as we needed for four small rucksacks and a blanket-size cover.

Our next stop was the cobblers' workshop, where we gathered enough long leather strips to make straps for our rucksacks. Then we took it all over to the shoemaker whose sign we had seen in the main street. There we explained that we had no money and asked him if he would sew the rucksacks together for us and fasten the straps to them.

He was a wizened little man with a drooping, nicotine-coloured moustache. For some time he looked at us in silence, then said, "You're some of those prisoners, aren't you?"

We nodded.

"All right," he said, "come back in a couple of hours and I'll have them ready for you." It was quite amazing how meek and helpful the Germans had suddenly become.

We met the self-styled prison director again, who seemed to have taken a special fancy to me and who made us thoroughly uncomfortable by inviting us in for coffee. We managed to squirm out of that one, but as we finally took our leave, he called me back, and before I knew it he had pressed into my hands two sheets of what he said were food coupons and some paper currency. I thanked him hurriedly and rejoined my friends as fast as I could. I had no idea what the fellow wanted from us, but his attitude was too smirking, his smile too cunning to be prompted by disinterested kindness. Rather he gave me the impression of a hairy black spider trying to weave a web around us.

Our all-knowing cook had bad news for us that day. "You've got to get out of here tomorrow," he advised us. "This prison is going to be used again and they want a couple of days to clean it out and clear away the wreckage."

We were quite indignant about this. "First you tell us to stay on here, and then you say we've got to get out in a day," we protested. "We can't leave tomorrow. We've got to take the patients to the hospital."

He looked at us quizzically. "I didn't say you had to get out of the town," he remarked, "just out of this prison. Why don't you billet yourselves somewhere in town? You'll be better off that way. Just register with the Russian Kommandant and he'll give you some food coupons and tell you where to go. Anyway, I've got some supplies here for you and you can come back tomorrow for some more, but that will be the last time I can give you a meal." He produced two one-pound cans of lard, two of ersatz jam, and a small bag of dried peas.

With that we retreated to discuss this latest development. All of us had lived illegally under the Nazi occupation and we automatically shied from registering anywhere. How could we know if registering with the Russian Kommandant wasn't the first step on the road of evacuation via Odessa, which we were so determined to avoid? "Anyway," I said, "I already have food coupons," and I pulled the two sheets out of my pocket. The others goggled, and I explained quickly how I had obtained them.

"You sure they're not false ones?" asked Dries sceptically.

"Search me," I said. "I don't trust the fellow any more than you do. The point is that if we leave the day after tomorrow, we don't have to use them, at least not in this town. We've got enough food now for a couple of days, especially if the cook still feeds us tomorrow." I also showed them the money. We examined it critically but had no way of telling whether it was valid, so we decided not to use it unless we had to and divided it up into four parts, each pocketing our share of twelve marks.

"Well, if we have to find a billet in the town for one night," said Nell, "we might as well find one for two. This prison gives me the creeps. Suppose they close the portal during the night and catch us inside; how are we going to convince them we don't belong here?"

Accordingly we set off to find a billet. We rang several door-bells along the street, but if a door opened at all, it was only at a crack, and as soon as we stated our mission, it was closed in our faces. This was getting us nowhere. We needed somebody in authority to blast the trail for us. "There's those French-women with their little lieutenant," suggested Joke. She was referring to a small group of French women politicals who had stayed behind and taken over the dormitory where our former guards had been billeted. They had somehow picked up a French lieutenant in full uniform, who now went around with them everywhere, swaggering and looking important. We had seen this little group around the town but had not had any dealings with them.

We found them easily enough—they were busy organising some sausages from a reluctant butcher—and the little lieutenant was only too happy at another chance to throw his weight around. He was one of those small fellows who had suffered agonies from being just a number in a POW camp, and was now getting his own back from the sense of power it gave him to be the only French lieutenant in a defeated enemy town. His power was largely imaginary, but he hadn't discovered this yet, and his uniform might just do the trick so far as we were concerned. We picked the biggest house on the town square and let the lieutenant do the talking for us, in badly fractured but very authoritative German. It seemed to work. The German owners were none too happy about it, but the uniform had the right effect; they agreed to let us have a small maid's room on the top floor.

Very pleased, we thanked the lieutenant and went to get our belongings. On the way we picked up our rucksacks. The shoemaker had done a very nice job; the seams were doubly sewed, and the straps securely attached; he had even put in some eyeholes for the drawstrings. We gave him two of our cigars and he was so delighted that he practically bowed us out of the door. Yet, for all we knew, the cigars could have been stolen from him in the first place.

Carefully we packed our supplies—blankets and other odd belongings—into the rucksacks and the Pram and presented ourselves at our new quarters. But we had been too trusting. The German owners had not sat still during our absence; they had procured a uniform of their own. They opened the door to us all right, but only to show us a Russian soldier standing in their hallway. He was a tall fellow who looked thoroughly bored and did not even listen to all the excited talk that burst out in front of him. If he had been American, he would have been chewing gum. Being Russian, he waited in stolid silence while the Germans scoldingly told us we had no right to impose on them; then he stuck out a huge paw with a small piece of paper in it. It proved to be a note from the Kommandant's office which said, in German, that we could not take billets without his approval and that we had to register first. We would gladly have kicked those fat Germans up and down their big house, but knowing well enough that we were defeated, we turned around without a word. Evidently we had picked on the one German family that, for some reason, had enough pull with the Russians to get the busy Kommandant to come to their rescue. And there we were, in the middle of the town square with our pitiful luggage, and no place to go except back to prison.

"Let's try again," said Dries. "If we go back to that prison I'll die. There must be some place in this town where we can sleep. We're not asking much."

Silently all of us agreed we couldn't live behind bars any more; we would rather sleep in the middle of the square. We tried some more doorbells on that side of the square, but the doors stayed shut, so we trundled our little wagon to the other side, where the French politicals and the lieutenant had their dormitory. Maybe people on this side were more used to prisoners. Maybe this lawyer, whose nameplate was next to his bell, would have some understanding of the justice of our request. We were just talking to keep one another's hopes up. None of us really believed any more that we would find a roof over our heads in these middle-class homes, and I was already weighing in my mind the possibility of holing up in the abandoned dairy plant at the other side of the town—if it was still abandoned. We hadn't checked up on it since the buttermilk ran out. No doubt the others were turning over similar schemes in their minds. Nevertheless we rang the lawyer's bell.

The door was opened by a motherly-looking woman between fifty and sixty. Very politely we explained our request: we only wanted to stay two nights; we were Hollanders and we wouldn't make a mess or steal anything; we wouldn't ask her for food; we had been political prisoners, not criminals; wouldn't her husband recognise that we had some rights? "My husband isn't at home," she said hesitantly. But we renewed our chorus, and after some more wavering she gave in and led us to a long, narrow room at the back of the house. The room had two beds, fully made up. It was much better than the maid's room we had been offered before. "This is where our daughters sleep when they come home for the holidays," said the woman, "but they are in Kassel and we haven't heard from them for months. This war has been so terrible."

She looked like somebody's grandmother and if she hadn't been German, I would have kissed her.

"It's going to be better from now on," I ventured.

She looked at me with beseeching eyes. "Do you think so?" she sighed, "do you really think so?"

It occurred to me, briefly, that maybe for her it wasn't going to be better, but I thrust the thought firmly aside. We had no time for sentimentalities. Quickly and efficiently we brought our luggage in, before she could change her mind. She hovered around. Our plan for that afternoon, before we heard about the prison's being reactivated, had been to find a Protestant minister to keep an eye on our three patients after our departure. I did not know whether our temporary hostess was religious, much less whether she was Catholic or Protestant, but I knew that this was a generally Protestant part of Germany and decided to have a try. "We would like to talk to the *Pfarrer*," I said. "Could you tell us where to find him?"

It had been a haphazard arrow, but it found its mark. She beamed suddenly and bustled off to find us the address. She returned with a printed card of the minister's name and explained how we could find the house where he lived.

From there on, she trusted us and left us alone.

The minister proved to be a portly man with a florid face and a brisk way of speaking. As I sat in his stuffy parlour, watching him while Nell explained about our three sick ex-prisoners in the hospital and asked him to go to see them and make sure that they got proper care, I reflected that if I were one of the sick I would not be particularly pleased to see this man at my bedside. There was no compassion in his face as he listened to Nell, and it did not seem to upset him that in the prison so near his church people had been treated in such a thoroughly un-Christian manner. I had to restrain myself from asking him if he had ever tried to visit the prisoners or arrange a service for them, or whether he knew how many had died there from starvation while he had been eating so well that his black waistcoat strained at the buttons. But even if he wasn't the kind of man we had hoped for, it was still a good idea to make him aware of the existence of our patients—and of the fact that we planned to give the Red Cross his name in case they needed his assistance. But I was glad when we had written down the three names for him and the interview was over, and not at all surprised when, as he showed us out, his hand was already at shoulder height and the word *"Heil"* had popped out of his mouth, before he remembered that *"Heil Hitler"* might not be the best way to address us and swallowed the rest.

Fafa laughed when we told her about him, in the prison hospital where we had gone to tell her the adventures of the day. "Don't worry," she said. "If and when he comes to see me, I'll have some questions ready for him and I'll enjoy seeing him squirm." We marvelled at her cheerfulness and courage. She even had a good influence on the other two patients, who for the first time showed some interest in what was going on around them. I had my doubts that either of them would survive. They were no more than living skeletons and their eyes burned with fever. But we cheered them up as best we could and carefully took down their addresses, names of family to be informed, and various other data, and promised that we would let the Red Cross know about them as soon as we could find a Red Cross officer.

Our first night of sleeping behind windows without bars and in regular beds was not an unqualified success. Joke, who shared a bed with Dries, tossed and turned for a while, then resolutely climbed out, put a blanket on the floor, and contentedly rolled herself in another blanket on top of it. "That bed is too damn' soft!" she said. We laughed at her, but before the night was over I had joined her on the floor. Apparently it would take some time before our bodies could get used to spring mattresses again.

At the civilian hospital the next morning, it turned out that the doctor had been as good as his word. The admission personnel were expecting us; they provided us with an operation-room stretcher, mounted on wheels. We spent half the day pushing this conveyance between the prison and the hospital, moving our three patients and their few belongings. At last we had them installed in good hospital beds, in bright and clean rooms. To my relief, Fafa got a room to herself. The other two were together in a room with french windows opening onto a small balcony; they would get plenty of fresh air. I knew that Fafa, like the rest of us, must be pretty well immune to tuberculosis if she hadn't caught it by now, but, even so, it seemed to me she would be better off without the constant threat of a contagious disease around her. There were tears in her eyes when we said good-bye, but her jauntiness never left her. "I may be home before you," she joked. "Just tell the Red Cross to come for me with an aeroplane."

It was past one o'clock when we arrived at the prison for our last meal there, and the cook was impatiently waiting for us at the portal. "Thought you would never come," he grumbled as he preceded us to the kitchen. "They could come and close this place any time now. They've already put new prisoners in the back wing. I finally persuaded those Frenchmen to get out. They wouldn't believe me till they saw the prisoners being brought in." We knew that he had been feeding the two groups

of Frenchmen as well as us, but, although we had speculated
about it often, we never could understand the almost fatherly
interest the fellow took in us. Our best guess was that, as a
Communist, he had been a prisoner at one time or another and
therefore knew how we felt. That still didn't explain how he
had suddenly turned up here as the new prison cook and why
he had not been in a concentration camp till the end of the war,
like all other Communists. It was evident from his stocky, well-
fed appearance that if he had been a prisoner it had not been
recently. But he had made it clear that he disliked personal
questions and we knew better than to ask him.

While we were gratefully spooning up the thick pea-soup he
served us, I inquired casually, not really expecting an answer,
"Who are these new prisoners? Are they all the big-shot
Nazis?"

To my surprise he gave a loud belly-laugh and answered,
"Sure, most of them are Nazis, but one of them is a friend of
yours." We looked up with plain disbelief and he chuckled.
"Remember that fellow who made out he was the new director? Well, they got him locked up now. He was just a black
marketeer who needed a new front and he tried to make this
prison his headquarters."

This time we laughed with him and I finally understood the
reason why the pseudo-director had thrust the money and food
coupons upon me. He had been a spider spinning his web all
right!

"You really planning to leave to tomorrow?" asked the cook.
When we assured him we were, he shook his head and said, "I
don't think they'll let you through, but you have my blessing.
I've got some more stuff for you." With that he brought out a
small saucepan, four loaves of bread, a half-pound bag of
sugar, a small piece of sausage, and a pound bag of groats. We
thanked him profusely and gave him our last two cigars, which
we had brought along for him. Then we all shook his hand and
said good-bye. We had grown quite fond of this enigmatic
little man, and our thanks were sincere; without him we would

have had a tough time finding enough food to keep us going and probably would have had to start our long trek home with empty hands.

Later that afternoon, as we passed the men's prison on our way to a half-burned-out sawmill near the hospital, where we hoped to find some rope to secure our luggage on the Pram, we saw that the doors of the big portal were closed. A new era had begun.

We were up bright and early the next morning. While Nell conscientiously stripped the beds and Joke prepared some bread and jam for each of us, Dries and I carefully loaded the Pram. We decided to put into it three blankets and two rucksacks full of supplies, and had found enough rope to tie them down securely. We would carry our other two rucksacks packed with the remaining two blankets, our underwear, and our embroideries. We planned that two of us would pull the Pram while the other two carried rucksacks till we were all ready to change places. We said a polite farewell to our hostess, carried the Pram outside with loving care, and found ourselves on the cobblestoned town square at 8 a.m. on May 17, 1945. We had been free for exactly ten days.

With Nell and Dries pulling the Pram and Joke and I carrying the rucksacks, we set out up the winding street that led north. But we did not get far. Even before we had reached the spot where the street changed into a gravel road, the Pram ignominiously keeled over and lost its left wheel, which went rolling off by itself till it hit the curb. For a moment we stood there, looking down on our crippled little wagon as if our fervent wishing could mend it. Then Dries heaved a deep sigh, let go with a string of choice seaman's curses, and asked, "Shall we try to carry it all or shall we abandon it?"

But Joke had been looking around. "We don't have to abandon it," she said. "Look, there's a blacksmith's shop right over there. Maybe we can get the Pram repaired." She was right. By sheer luck, our breakdown had come almost in front of the blacksmith's.

While Dries, Nell, and Joke carried our disabled Pram and the wayward wheel to our potential saviour. I rushed back into town. I had suddenly remembered that somewhere I had seen a store sign saying "Furniture and toys" and that maybe I could find something sturdier than our Pram. In my eager hurry I turned the wrong corner, and it was some time before I found the store. Then I burst in on the owner, who had just opened his shop. Disregarding him, I hunted through his wares till I found what I wanted: a small wagon, consisting of a simple wooden platform, about two feet by four, with four-inch walls around the sides and mounted on small wooden wheels. It was meant as a toy for small children: the wooden handle to pull it by ended with a crossbar at about the height of my knees. Seizing the little cart under my arm, I impatiently pulled my share of German notes from my pocket, pushed them into the store owner's hand, and galloped back to my friends with my new find. They were standing around the blacksmith's anvil, where mysterious things were being done to our Pram's under-carriage.

"Hey!" I yelled, "I've found a tank for us!"

But they were too fascinated by the work at the anvil and too deafened by the noise of it to notice me till, panting, I stood beside them. Then Joke awoke to the possibilities of my wagon and together we went outside and lashed half of our load to my "Tank". "That's a good name, Zip," Joke said gravely. "From here on we'll have a Tank and a Pram."

Eventually the blacksmith got the wheel fixed, and Dries gave him his share of German money. This time the Pram carried a lighter load. An extra piece of rope was attached to the handle of the Tank so that we could pull it without lifting the front wheels, and we set off once more. Dries and I pulled the Tank while Joke and Nell followed with the Pram. There were no sentries to challenge us. Laboriously we climbed the steep road north.

Even though we had eaten fairly regularly during the last ten days, we were acutely aware of our physical weakness during that climb. It was all we could do to reach the crest with our little wagons, and only our tremendous urge to be on our way made us go a little farther, over the crest and through the pine woods that covered it. At the edge of the wood we stopped. Before us lay a wide, rolling landscape, alive with ripening wheat and rye gently waving on the breeze, dotted with small farms off the road and spanned by a wide, sunny May sky speckled with small clouds sailing gaily off to no-where. Down a slope at our left cascaded a well-tended cherry orchard, and lining the road on our right stood a row of pear-trees, some still in late bloom.

We stood there as an overpowering feeling of freedom came surging over us. Waldheim had been a small town in a hollow; as long as we were still cooped up there, with the prison loom-ing large in our minds, we had only been half-free. Now, as we drank in the sunny openness of this peaceful-looking land, the immensity of freedom rolled over us like waves on an ocean beach, engulfing us, taking our breath away, making us teeter on our weak legs. We all felt like singing, crying, shouting, and laughing simultaneously, but for a long time we remained speechless and motionless.

Finally we stirred and discovered that the emotion had made us ravenously hungry. Far off, from the prison town that we had left, we could hear the church clock booming out the noon hour. We sat down under a pear-tree and had a picnic.

Chapter Four

OUR progress was slow. Light as they were the little wagons soon felt like dead weights pulling on our aching arms. We changed places often, from left to right or from the Tank to the Pram, to divide the load evenly among ourselves and between our right and left arms, but it wasn't long before all the muscles in our arms and shoulders seemed to be on fire. During the long months of imprisonment, in which an occasional shuffle around the yard had been our only exercise, our feet had grown tender; and now blisters began to form all over them. The sun was hot; thirst started to bother us. After about an hour we spied a small brook running through a field a hundred yards from the road. Leaving the wagons on the roadside, we rushed over and, lying flat on our stomachs, drank deeply from the clear, fast-running water. After plunging our heads in to wet our hair and necks, we lay there for a while, resting till we felt refreshed enough to pick up our loads again.

For the first two hours of the afternoon, we had the road to ourselves. There was no traffic whatsoever and we met nobody. Except for a plume of smoke rising from the chimney of a farm here and there, the country could have been deserted. We saw no farmers in the fields and no sign of the Red Army. Wherever the last fighting of this war had taken place, it had obviously not been in the sleepy countryside around us. Not a single tank track on the road or through the rich fields, not a shell-hole anywhere, not one burned-out farm-house.

Toward the end of the afternoon we came upon a small town. As in Waldheim, every house was decorated with a red flag, but there were few people in the streets and no traffic. We saw several Russian soldiers and a couple of sentries in front of the town hall, which had evidently been taken over by the Russians, but there seemed to be no big encampment. We walked proudly through the middle of the town—grateful for the short stretch of asphalt-paved street that made our wagons roll easier, and for the drinking-fountain in the square, where we slaked our thirst again—then out of it at the other end.

And there things changed. Deserted as the countryside had been at the other side of the town, here it was swarming with liberated Russian POWs and slave labourers. As we knew, the Nazis had used Russian and Polish POWs as slave labourers too, and the only difference between them was that the POWs wore remnants of a uniform while the slave labourers wore a wide variety of civilian clothes, many of them new and obviously liberated from their former bosses. Otherwise they all had round shaved heads and the gaunt, starved look of people who have done forced labour on a bare subsistence diet. But now they were happy and busy getting their own back. Unlike us, they were the same nationality as the occupying army and they could order the Nazis around to their hearts' content. We saw two of them swaggering up to a farm and reappearing shortly afterwards, each with a goose under his arm. We saw groups of them crowded into farm wagons drawn by horses, mules, or even oxen, singing gaily and waving bottles of schnapps. Many of them seemed to be staying in the neighbourhood, living off the land, enjoying their freedom and in no hurry to go home. Others, those in the farm wagons, were on their way in the same general direction as ours.

Soon one of the ex-slave labourers came up to us and, pointing at our wrists, said, *"Uhr, Uhr." Uhr* is German for watch; he wanted ours. Pulling up our sleeves we showed him that we hadn't any. This saddened him, but suddenly his face lit up and, pulling up his own sleeve, he displayed a dozen watches covering his arm from wrist to elbow. Generously he undid two straps and gave us two of them. We shook his hand, said "*Spasibo*" and continued on our way. We hadn't gone a mile before another Russian relieved us of our new riches.

It was near evening now and we figured we had covered about ten miles. Bone-tired, hungry, and stumbling on our blistered feet, we were ready to call it a day. Originally we had planned to sleep at the side of the road, but big thunder-clouds were piling up in the sky and we didn't enjoy the idea of getting drenched by a storm. Moreover, with all these liberated Russkis roaming the countryside, it seemed safer to find some kind of shelter. Accordingly we left the main road and guided our wagons along the ruts of a narrow lane leading to a cluster of small farm buildings. We found the farmer and his wife in their kitchen, fearfully watching our approach. But when they discovered that we only wanted to spend the night in their barn, they relaxed and even offered us the use of the kitchen stove.

While we were unpacking our supplies and blankets, a Russian sergeant in full uniform and carrying a tommy gun materialised from nowhere and stood watching us. We asked him in German if he had any objection to our being there. To our surprise he understood us and shook his head. Encouraged, we tried to start a conversation, but, though he seemed to catch the meaning of what we said, he wasn't capable of answering in more than a few broken words, or maybe he was being cagey. However, he taught us the word *njeponimai* for "I don't understand". He told us, too, that the Red Army was everywhere around us, and when I asked him if we could get milk anywhere, he pointed to another farm a little way off.

I promptly got out our small soup-pail and set out, but he called for me to wait and came with. For a moment I wasn't sure whether it wouldn't be wiser to turn back empty-handed. Maybe I was walking straight into a trap. But the sergeant had an open, trustworthy face and I could not bring myself to give up the promised milk so lightly. At the other farm several Russian soldiers were lounging in the courtyard. The sergeant gave a brisk command and one of them got up, took my pail, and went into the barn. He returned with the pail almost full of milk—at least three quarts of it. Then the sergeant, half with gestures, half in German, made it clear that I could come back the next morning at seven-thirty for more milk.

When I rejoined the others, I found that they had neatly arranged our quarters. On a thick layer of straw they had spread out the piece of canvas with our blankets on top. The Pram was parked in a corner and the Tank had been turned upside down to form a low table on which were laid out our mugs, spoons, saucepan, and bread and lard.

While we sat down to drink a mug of milk, the farmer and his wife, who had scurried back into their kitchen as soon as the Russian sergeant appeared, came out again and eagerly asked me, "Did they rape you?"

I laughed and answered, "No, they were very polite and friendly."

Thereupon they broke into a long lament about how terrible it was to have these Russians around. Scores of girls and women had been raped; the soldiers were looting everywhere; this shouldn't happen to poor innocent people like them. We paid no attention, and Nell put an end to it by picking up the bag of groats, the remainder of the milk, and the saucepan, and announcing that she would now like to use the kitchen stove. They escorted her inside. Shortly afterwards Nell reappeared with a delicious hot mixture of milk, groats, and honey. She had wheedled the honey from the farmer's wife and also obtained the loan of four soup-plates. We sat cross-legged around the upturned Tank and had a king-size meal. After that we barely had enough strength left to stagger to the pump and wash our dishes before we stretched our tired limbs on the springy softness of the straw and immediately dropped off to sleep.

Joke awoke first and hurried over to the kitchen to see what

F

time it was. Then she prodded me, saying, "Wake up, Zip, you have to get the milk!"

We had slept fully dressed. Now I pulled off my sweater and washed under the pump till the grogginess of sleep had left me. Then I picked up the pail and gaily set off through the orchard to the other farm. The grass and the branches of the trees were dripping wet but the sun was shining brightly. A heavy storm must have broken during the night, although I had heard none of it, and now the whole world around me sparkled with freshness. Again I felt my heart swell with the great wonder of being free.

Our Russian sergeant was even better than his word. Not only did he fill my pail with milk again, he also gave me five eggs! While I thanked him, he touched the little flag on my sweater and raised his eyebrows in a question. "Holland," I said. He looked blank. I tried "*Hollandski*" and "*Netherlandski*," but it was no use. Either he had never heard of my country or the Russians had a completely different name for it. The former was more likely than the latter, I reflected, as I walked slowly back, carrying the pail in one hand and a kerchief full of eggs in the other. After all, why should a young, handsome inhabitant of the great vastness that was Russia know about a tiny, overcrowded country on the North Sea, unless his schoolteachers had told him about Peter the Great's going there to learn shipbuilding? Would schoolteachers in a Communist country still be allowed to reveal such facts, and, if they did, had our sergeant, who looked about twenty-three, had time enough to absorb all the teaching he could get before he was drafted into the army?

Still musing about these things, I found my three friends happily splashing water on each other around the pump. Now Nell took charge again. She let each of us have a drink of milk from the pail, then disappeared with it and the eggs into the kitchen. While we were waiting for her, the farmer and his wife visited us again and started their complaint anew. Finally Dries interrupted to ask them what they had lost. "Well," they

said, "the Russians have taken two mattresses and two comforters, and our big clock, and a bag of wheat and a goose, and
we have to keep our two daughters inside for fear they will be
raped."

At this point Joke couldn't contain herself any longer, "Do
you realise how you Germans have plundered Holland?" she
asked hotly. "You talk about one goose and a couple of mattresses. You think there are any geese left in Holland? Or any
wheat? No, there aren't! Your Nazis have stripped our country
more thoroughly than anything the Russians have done here so
far. They've taken our food, our bicycles, the machinery from
our factories, the livestock from our farms, our wheat, our
sugar-beets, even the sleepers of our railways!" She stopped for
breath and, red in the face, resumed—"You've made slave
labour or prisoners out of a whole generation of youngsters"—
then realised that her audience had left.

"Keep your shirt on, Joke," said Dries kindly. "You were
right in saying so, they had a lesson coming to them; but forget
about it now. Don't poison your own mind with these things.
Look, the sun is shining and we're free, kid, we're free!" Joke
hugged him and got her smile back, and Nell came out of the
kitchen with a steaming pan. This time her concoction of groats
tasted even better, for she had beaten an egg into it. We had
two platefuls each and after that we didn't even want any
bread. Nell had wisely hard-boiled the other four eggs so that
we could have them for lunch, and we cheerfully set about
loading the wagons. Our hosts had withdrawn into the inner
chambers of their farm and we didn't bother to say good-bye.
It was eight-forty-five by the kitchen clock when we headed
for the main road again.

Surprisingly, we were not stiff at all. The sound sleep had
taken the ache out of our muscles and we all felt fit and ready
to tackle the world, except for our blistered feet. But again luck
was with us. We had hardly gone half a mile along the main
road when, from a farm that bordered the road, a small wagon
drawn by a single horse turned into it. Riding in the wagon

were two Russian ex-POWs. They saw us, waited for us, and with many gestures and a lot of laughing invited us to tie our little wagons to theirs and climb aboard. No invitation could have been more welcome; we gratefully accepted.

And there we were, seated comfortably on their wagon, keeping an eye on the Tank and the Pram, slowly jogging along. The horse could have been a Waldheim prisoner—he was just as much skin-over-bones as we, and all he could manage was a slow step. But the ride spared our blisters and gave us time to enjoy the antics of a lot of Russians careering along the road on liberated bicycles, which they were quite obviously riding for the first time in their lives. After a while the driver turned round and passed us a box of small strong-smelling cheeses. Life was getting better and better! A few pieces were missing from the box, but we counted the rest and there were forty of them left. So we munched cheese, contentedly basking in the sunshine and occasionally breaking into song, to the great pleasure of our Russian friends. Once, to let the horse drink, we stopped at a farm where a dozen ex-slave labourers had made their quarters. One of them, clad only in a white shirt, was determinedly trying to ride a bike around the cobblestone courtyard. He would get on it, go a few wildly swaying yards, fall off, pick himself up, get on again. His comrades were shouting encouragement, dodging and scurrying in all directions to keep out of his way. From our perch on the wagon we watched this happy horseplay, laughing till the tears stood in our eyes.

Towards-noon our two Russian friends decided that maybe their horse would go a little faster if it had a lighter load to pull, and they signalled us to get off. However, to show that their good will hadn't changed, they went into the nearest farm and returned with a jug of milk. They filled our mugs, and we toasted them in milk, then unhitched the Tank and the Pram, and set off on foot once again, waving good-bye to our benefactors, who slowly disappeared from sight in their creaking wagon.

Now that we were walking again, practically every Russian we met stopped us to ask for "*Uhr, Uhr*," but, as we were again watchless, we couldn't satisfy their urgent demands. They didn't hold it against us. As soon as we had pulled up our sleeves and shown our bare arms, most of them would clap us gaily on the shoulder and we would all continue on our way. But one of them had a real problem. After he was convinced that we had no watch to give him, he showed us the armful that he had already collected, shook them, held them up to his ear, said "*Kaput, nyet*" and turned up his palms in a gesture of hopelessness. None of his watches was going! With some careful persuasion, we got him to take them all off and started to wind them for him, showing him how to go about it. We left him standing in the middle of the road, slowly moving his arm past his ear, from wrist to elbow and back, listening to the ticking of his watches with a look of pure rapture on his face.

We passed through another small town, called Ostra. Dries, after consulting his map, decided that our progress was satisfactory and that we could afford a long rest. We had walked about two and a half hours, judging by the sun, and when we came to a bridge crossing a small brook, we left the road and followed the brook upstream a little way till we came to the perfect picnic place, a natural water-hole surrounded by trees and with a grassy clearing on one side. Unable to resist the temptation, Joke and I immediately stripped and slid into the water for a delightful swim, while Dries and Nell kept watch on the bank. Then we had a lunch of hard-boiled eggs with cheese and bread, and stretched out in the grass for a nap.

"This is living," said Dries, with wonder and gratitude in his voice. "A month ago I didn't even dare dream this would ever happen to me again."

We all felt the same. It was true that we were outlaws, without any means of proving our identity, far away from homes which might not even exist now, living by our wits in a country shaken by the chaos of defeat, but we were free and we were happy. And we soon found that even some of our former enemies shared our feelings. As we were refastening the luggage before returning to the road, a man on crutches came limping through the field behind us. To our surprise he was wearing a German uniform coat, stripped of all insignia, and German fatigue trousers. He was the only German soldier we had set eyes on since the prison doors were opened, and we were curious enough to ask him how he happened to turn up here. His story was quite simple. He had been on the Russian front, and during the painful retreat of his unit, through Russia and Poland, one of his feet had frozen. (It was still wrapped in rags.) About a month ago he had finally been evacuated to a German hospital not far from Ostra, which was his home town. The day before, he had seen his way clear and had merely limped out and away; he had taken to the back roads to regain his home, which he had now nearly reached. "Boy, am I glad this dirty war is over!" he exulted. We couldn't agree more. When we told him we were on our way to Riesa, he advised us to follow the brook a little farther upstream. There we would find the back road that he had just come from, which would save us at least a mile on our trek.

We followed his directions. The back road was no more than a path, but it was wide enough for the Tank and the Pram, and the natural soil was kinder on our feet than the gravel road. We set off once more, delighted with our surroundings. On our right the water of another brook laughed happily, coursing over round shiny boulders. At times we would pass through small woods where the sunlight filtered through in greenish-gold patches and the air was perfumed with the scent of lilacs and hawthorn. At other times the landscape would open up into wide, rolling fields, and we passed many prosperous-looking farms with well-tended flower gardens. We had the path to ourselves, and without the interruptions from Russians who wanted watches we were making good headway. Passing through a village, we were hailed by two young women sitting in a small front garden. We stopped and learned that the women had fled their homes in Silesia two months ago and wanted to know whether we came from the same direction, for they hadn't had any news from their town. We answered that we were Hollanders on our way home and that we probably knew even less about what was going on than they did. Thereupon they told us that a group of twenty Dutch ex-POWs had come through there a couple of days earlier and that they had been well received in the castle of Ragewitz, some three miles farther. At the mention of a castle, Joke and I, who were in front with the Pram, pricked up our ears. "Come on, Baron," we called to Nell. "We're going to do things in style. We'll sleep in a real castle tonight."

But Nell and Dries persuaded us to wait. One of the two refugee women had disappeared into the house and Nell said she was fetching some food for us. Joke and I were impatient, but the wait proved worth while, for the women returned with four heads of lettuce and a quarter pound of real coffee beans, something we hadn't seen for years. We thanked them sincerely and started off with new energy, this time in search of a castle.

We found it easily enough—an enormous, imposing building situated in a kind of park and surrounded by several clusters of farm buildings. The park bordered on our path; as we went into it we hesitated. We saw three marble steps leading to a huge oaken door adorned with brass knockers. Did we really dare go up there, dirty and shabby as we were? We decided it wouldn't hurt to try, so we carried our little wagons up the marble steps and knocked boldly. After a little while the big door was opened a crack and we were face to face with a very old, grey-haired gentleman.

Briefly we explained who we were, that we had heard that Hollanders had been welcome here before, and could we please spend the night?

The door opened wide. "Of course, of course," said the old gentleman. "I cannot offer you much, but at least I can give

you a roof over your heads." He led us into an impressive
marble hall and called for his wife, an old lady who promptly
came shuffling out of one of the many doorways. She explained
that all the bedrooms were occupied because so many members of her large family had sought refuge in the old castle
during the closing months of the War, but that if we would be
satisfied with a couch, we were quite welcome. With that she
opened another door and led us into a big sunny room.

We gasped. It was more a hall than a room. A banquet of
fifty people could easily have taken place here, with plenty of
space left for a dozen butlers to hurry about. The far wall was
made up entirely of huge bay windows lined with comfortable-
looking window seats. The other walls were hung with life-size
portraits of ancestors arrayed in the splendour of eighteenth-
and nineteenth-century dress. A huge Persian rug covered the
middle of the shiny parquet floor, and I counted among the
furniture three davenports and a grand piano, almost lost in all
this space.

The old lady stood by with a quiet smile while we took it
all in, secretly struggling to regain our breath and some of our
old assurance. Now she took Nell's hand and said, "Come, I'll
show you the kitchen." We all trooped after them, meeting
several other elderly people in the marble hall. The kitchen
was big and cool and old-fashioned, with lots of shiny copper-
ware hanging on the walls. We asked if we could get any milk
from the adjoining farms. "You will have to ask the Russians,"
said the old lady. "They have taken over all the farms. We have
to beg from them, too."

Next she showed us a lavatory and then left us to ourselves.
All four of us had the same reaction: we instantly set about
washing, combing our tousled hair, and generally making ourselves as presentable as we could, even though we couldn't
possibly hope to live up to the magnificence of our quarters. I
set off with the pail to see what could be found on the farms. At
the first one I had no luck. There was nobody around but two
Russian soldiers who didn't understand what I wanted, and

didn't try, either. But at the next farm I found a Russian who spoke fairly good German and who seemed to have assumed the same kindness as the castle owners. He filled my pail with milk, gave me six eggs and six big potatoes, which I wrapped in the kerchief I had bought along, and, to top it all off, he added a handful of Russian cigarettes. I hurried back with my bounty, and, while Dries and I smoked long-filtered cigarettes on the window seat, Nell and Joke repaired to the kitchen.

It was quarter-past seven by the ornate Empire clock on the wall of our banquet hall when we sat down on straight-backed chairs at a big round table to have our most elaborate meal yet. Nell had been given vinegar, thyme, parsley, chives, and tarragon by one of the kind old ladies she met in the kitchen, and we did ourselves proud with an *omelette aux fines herbes*, fresh salad, parsley potatoes, mugs of milk, and cheese and real coffee for dessert. Joke had borrowed plates and forks from the kitchen and, half unconsciously, we were all trying to sit up straight and mind our table manners. Even so, we felt that all the proud ancestors along the walls were frowning down upon us, tut-tutting among themselves and wondering what their once distinguished family had come to if four tramps like these were allowed to set foot in the hallowed hall. When Dries started to spear a piece of cheese on his knife, but changed his mind and delicately juggled it out of the box and onto his plate with a spoon and fork, we all went into a fit of giggles and didn't sober up again till we started to discuss our hosts.

"They must all be counts and countesses," said Joke. "They address each other with some kind of title."

"I'm sure they are," said Nell. "What's more, one of those old ladies in the kitchen told me that her son and her nephew had been prisoners too, but that they were now free. I asked her where they had been prisoner, thinking they had been POWs, but she said right here in Germany. She also mentioned July the twentieth and then she hurried away. What do you think she meant?"

"July the twentieth!" said Dries excitedly. "That was the

day of that bomb plot against Hitler that failed. Maybe they were connected with it in some way. That would explain why they are all holed up here and why they are being so kind to us."

We could only speculate. In the world we were living in one didn't ask questions, and the only information available was the kind that was volunteered freely. But we liked the theory; from there on we considered our nameless hosts secret comrades-in-arms.

After we had washed our dishes and returned the borrowed crockery to the kitchen, we huddled on the window seats, watching the slow change from day into dusk. Dries said, "Sing to me, will you? It'll make me feel more at home." The three of us started harmonizing. We liked to sing, and all our songs had special meanings for us: this was the one we made up just after we were condemned to death; this one was our signature tune for the parachute agent who had a cell along the same wing in Utrecht—it meant that we had some message for him and that he had to watch out for it; this was the one we sang in Düsseldorf while the town was being bombed at night by the RAF and we hoped that the prison walls would crack so that we could escape. We explained it all to Dries.

Then there was a knock on our door, and filing in came a good-looking red-haired woman of about thirty-five followed by four red-haired girls ranging from about fifteen to eight years old. "Please excuse us for disturbing you," said the woman, "but we heard your singing and my daughters and I would very much like to listen to you from close by. There is so little distraction for us these days. Please do go on singing."

We felt slightly embarrassed, but we could not refuse their request. The five of them arranged themselves on the floor and the window seats around us, and we resumed our concert. All our songs were in Dutch, English, and French, and they could not understand a word. They just seemed to enjoy the music and the gaiety. At times the girls would ask for an explanation of the lyrics; whenever our own version was too violently anti-

German or too ribald, we would by unspoken common accord revert to the original lyrics or, with such songs as "Praise the Lord and Pass the Ammunition," even tone down the originals a little. It seemed too cruel to let four little girls realise the hatred we still felt toward the nation that they undoubtedly loved. Dries did marvellously well in these free translations, and we soon left the job to him. As dusk turned to dark we were still singing. One of the girls had got up and turned on two lamps at the far end of the room and, on a quiet command of her mother's, taken a folding cot out of one of several closets and set it up next to the grand piano, but then she came back and snuggled up to Dries's legs and asked us to sing another song and still another.

Finally, the mother asked us the question we had dreaded from the start: Didn't we know any German songs?

This put us in a quandary. Practically the only German songs we knew were those that had been dinned into our ears by German soldiers marching through the streets of our home towns. Often we had been awakened at dawn, when a squad of singing soldiers returned from the dirty business of executing a member of the resistance. We knew the songs all right, but we would have been quartered alive rather than sing them. Nell rescued us. From her long experience with boy scouts she remembered several *Wandervögel* (hiking-club) songs and kept proposing them till she hit on one we all knew and had no objection to. The title was *"Die Gedanken sind frei"*, meaning "Thoughts are free", and we sang it with feeling. In the dim light I even imagined I saw a responsive wink from the mother, but I couldn't be sure. They left after this, each of the four daughters solemnly shaking our hands and making a little curtsey for each of us.

Wearily we unrolled our blankets and bedded down—Dries, Nell, and I on a davenport each, and Joke on the folding cot. We were almost asleep when Joke said, rather plaintively, "I don't know what to think. A month ago these Nazis were kicking us around, stealing our food, and treating us like vermin. Tonight we get curtsies from four nicely-brought-up girls, and they like our singing. It doesn't make sense."

I waited for Dries or Nell to give an answer, but they were either as dumbfounded as Joke or already sound asleep, so I ventured an answer of my own: "Don't worry, Joke, you can never generalise about a whole nation. There are bound to be exceptions, and tonight we seem to have met some of the exceptions. Maybe these are the people who will rebuild the kind of Germany we could live with, a democratic Germany."

"Well, they were nice girls," said Joke in a small, sleepy voice. "But what can little girls do about rebuilding Germany? I just hope they won't get raped by the Russians."

"Amen," growled Dries from his davenport.

The red-haired woman and her daughters came to see us off the next morning. She asked about our plans; when we told her that we were looking for a boat, she wrote down the addresses of several people in Riesa who might be able to help us. The two elder daughters accompanied us for half an hour, insisting on pulling the Tank for us. The castle was only about five miles from Riesa; for the first stretch we could still follow the pleasant path along the brook.

We met two French ex-prisoners going in the opposite direction and sat down with them to exchange news. They came from a prison east of Riesa and, after hiking to Riesa, had spent more than a week there trying to get on a train to the west. But it was no use, they said. No trains were leaving and the roads to the west were closed off. There were many former prisoners and slave labourers in the town and the Russians had set up a camp across the Elbe to collect them all. The rumour was that they were going to evacuate them through Odessa. As the Frenchmen were no more eager for that trip than we were, they had decided to try their luck farther south. We told them that farther south the situation was the same, including the talk about Odessa. They shrugged and said, "Well, maybe we can get out through Czechoslovakia. There must be some way to get out of here without making a detour over the Black Sea."

So we said good-bye; they went south and we continued north. Like the mice in one of those mazes built by scientists, we were all looking for an exit, blindly feeling our way without any rules or information to guide us, each jealously guarding his own plan, which he was sure would succeed.

After our path had rejoined the main road, we met many more of our colleagues going south. There was a gay group of Yugoslavs with a small covered wagon which they had decorated with flowering branches and an enormous flag. Next came five singing Italians. Then three Czechs, two men and a woman. We were still chatting with the Czechs, who told us that the Russians were getting difficult in Riesa and that everybody had to register and carry a pass, when, a little ahead of us, we saw a Russian ex-POW come out of a farm-house, proudly pushing a bicycle. We all watched him mount it, fall down, get on again, and move off, swaying crazily from one side of the road to the other. A little later, around a bend in the road, we came upon him sitting disconsolately under a tree with the bike in front of him. In one of his falls, one pedal had been pushed sideways so that it wouldn't move. We turned the bike upside down and, with a little pushing and pulling and a stout branch for a lever, soon had the pedal moving freely; we presented the bike to him with a flourish. He was radiant, shook hands all round, and wobbled off. He did better this time, and we were almost ready to believe that he had mastered the art when we saw him again, waiting at the side of the road. He had learned one thing, though; he had turned the bicycle upside down, ready for us to start the repairs. With a confident grin on his face he waved and shouted at us to hurry up and help him, and we found him completely irresistible.

Investigating, we discovered that the chain had come off. Since that wasn't too hard to fix either, we soon had the bike ready for him again. But the road started to go slightly uphill and we tried to tell him with gestures that it would be better for him to push to the top and not to get on till he was on the downgrade. Either this was too complicated or he was too impatient for such prudent tactics. At any rate he mounted again and smashed into a tree about a hundred yards farther on. Fortunately the bicycle held up this time and, after a joyous wave at us to show that all was well, he rode off once more, and we lost sight of him.

Shortly afterward we topped the rise ourselves and stood for a moment taking in the view. Before us lay the wide, flat, rich Elbe valley, and about a mile away, with the white ribbon of the road leading straight to it, was the town of Riesa, a shimmer of the river visible between the green pastures at its right and left. In front of the town and to the left of the road stood several long rectangular structures which we recognised as military barracks, and way ahead of us on the road, pedalling with crazy speed and weaving only slightly, was our Russian cyclist.

Cheered by the sight of our first goal, we started downhill. Just before we got to the barracks we met three other Hollanders, young boys of sixteen, seventeen, and nineteen, who told us that they had been picked off the streets of Rotterdam in January 1945 for slave labour in a factory near Riesa, and had been free since May third but unable to move. They had walked north first, had finally found a goods train that seemed to be headed west, and had slipped into an empty boxcar. But after a day and a night of shuttling and shunting they had found themselves back where they came from, in Riesa. Now they were going to try their luck south.

It was no use trying to dissuade them by telling them our own experience. We had paid very little attention to the railways—simply because we were convinced that they weren't running—and these boys still thought that the goods trains were their best chance. But all three looked pale and thin, and they had only one little knapsack among them, so we knew they must be hungry. The least we could do was offer them lunch. We sat down in the grass beside the road and shared the bottle of milk, the hard-boiled eggs we had brought along that morning, and the last of our bread.

While we were eating, a long column of Russian soldiers came marching out of the plain behind us and passed us on their way to the barracks in front of the town. They marched five abreast, practically filling the road, and so closely behind each other that if they hadn't kept step in perfect unison they would have stumbled over one another's heels. And all the way they sang. It was the first time we had seen our Russian allies in any kind of military formation and, especially after the carefree antics of most of the Russians we had met so far, it was a truly impressive showing. But we had little taste for military prowess; what really moved us was their singing. In that wide, open plain their virile voices rang out in such magnificent harmony, and with such sheer joy and pride, that our hearts couldn't help responding to it. We looked at each other with tears in our eyes and smiles on our lips, and were suddenly and inexorably convinced that life was full of beauty and purpose and promise.

The long column finally dissolved into the barracks buildings. Slowly we got up. As a farewell gift we presented the Dutch boys with our box of cheese, keeping four pieces for ourselves. They set off southward and we drew our little wagons into the town.

Compared with the small provincial towns we had seen so far, Riesa was quite a big place, swarming with former prisoners and slave labourers, with Russian soldiers of all ranks and, to our pleasant surprise, British POWs. We hailed the first Tommy we met, who agreeably told us the details. There had been a British POW camp at the outskirts of Riesa and that was where he had been since he had been caught in France in June 1940. The Russians had kept them there for a week after their liberation, but since then they had been free to roam around the town as they wanted. "Quite the life," he remarked. "The Jerries are now delighted to have us. Sort of protectors, you know. They don't trust these Russian chaps." However, he said the British POWs never strayed too far from their camp, for arrangements were now being made for all of them to be flown back to England and he, for one, wasn't going to miss that plane. This was the first news we had of any established link with the West; after the depressing information we had received from our colleagues on the road, it cheered us up considerably. We set off towards the river, and found two well-appointed club-houses, with spacious boat-houses attached. The first one belonged to the canoe club, but the club-house was a shambles of broken doors, windows, and furniture, and of the canoes little more was left than great mounds of splinters and strips of rubber. At the rowing club next door the same spectacle presented itself. The club looked as if a tornado had ripped through it, and in the boat-house we found rows and rows of beautiful skiffs, wherries, and racing shells, each one with great gaping rifle-butt holes in its sides. There were about thirty boats; any of more than a dozen of them would have suited our purpose, but not a single one was in floating condition. Even the light dinghy attached to the dock had been sunk with bullet holes in its bottom; we discovered it only because its rope was still attached to one of the landing poles.

Saddened, we turned back towards the town. It was now quite obvious that we would not find a boat as easily as we had hoped, and that we would need a place to stay till we did. Pulling our wagons and suddenly very aware of our tired muscles and our aching feet, we set out for an address on the list given us by the red-haired lady of the castle. It proved to be a fairly big house, surrounded by a well-tended garden. After insistent bell-ringing a servant appeared. She promptly closed the door in our faces, but she must have understood when we shouted "Ragewitz Castle," for after more bell-ringing she returned, this time with the lady of the house. Before we had finished our first sentence, the lady's strident voice poured over us a shrill recital of complaints about her hard life and we knew that it was futile to argue. We retreated to the pavement and walked a little way without a word. Then Dries exploded. "God damn it, if only I had a Russian uniform,

I'd make that woman jump through all the windows of her house!"

"How can she possibly be a friend of the lady of the castle?" mused Joke.

"Let's go and sleep in the boat-house," I proposed. "There's room enough, and we can fix a corner for ourselves. I'm tired of begging from these Nazis."

But Nell disagreed. "That's no good," she said. "This town is full of soldiers and there isn't a single door in either of those boat-houses and club-houses that closes. We may have to stay here several days and we'd better find a place where our stuff is safe. We've got one more address. Let's try it."

She was right; after looking up the street name, we kept asking for it till we were finally steered to the right place. It was after 7 p.m. when we arrived at the modest-looking house, but I was immediately hopeful when I saw by the nameplate that this was the house of a doctor. My own father was a general practitioner; maybe that introduction would work. But no introduction was necessary. A tall, grey-haired man with a young but lined face opened the door and listened to us in complete silence. When we were finished he said, "I'm sorry, my house is already quite full of refugees. However, if you don't mind taking the waiting-room——"

The waiting-room was a square, bare room, its only furniture four high-backed benches. It had two muslin-curtained windows looking on a small back yard. It also had three doors. One led to the vestibule through which we had come. Another led to a small adjoining lavatory and washroom, which the doctor said we could use, though he warned that there would be other people using it. The third door remained shut for the time being. After the doctor had left us, we surveyed our surroundings and found little to cheer about. "We'd better tie those benches together," said Nell. "They're too narrow to sleep on alone." Always practical, she had found something for us to do, and we set about untying our luggage from the Tank and the

G

Pram to find some odds and ends of string that we had packed in one of the rucksacks.

Before we were half done, the doctor's wife appeared to offer us a welcome and to give us a big cake of soap, four tooth-brushes, and a tube of toothpaste. This was a real godsend. Up to this time we had attempted to keep clean with some dried-out ersatz soap that we had found in our luggage, some very ancient toothbrushes, and no toothpaste at all. We left the Pram half untied and crowded into the washroom for a thorough clean-up. The doctor's wife seemed amused by this. She returned a little later with four cups of steaming coffee, a mixture of ersatz and the real stuff, which we gratefully gulped down. She had barely left when the third door opened and an elderly woman in a dirty kimono appeared. She surveyed us haughtily, dashed into the lavatory, returned, and at once be-came quite chatty, wanting to know everything about us. At first we answered only in monosyllables and wished heartily that she would leave us alone. But after she had darted back four times to the third door and produced, for brief and em-barrassed appearances, a cat, two teen-age daughters, and an incredibly shaggy dog, all the time telling a breathless story about how her house had been bombed in Cologne, we realised that she was not quite responsible and had to be humoured. After she had left, while we were tying the benches together, we christened her "Mrs Nut".

We were tired and hungry, but we had no bread left and no place to cook the dried peas, which would take hours to soften up, anyway. Just as we were discussing eating some spoonfuls of jam and keeping our four pieces of cheese for the morning, the third door opened again and Mrs Nut sailed in regally, carrying a dish of noodles. Behind her were several other refugees, all looking rather sheepish, but carrying more food: a saucepan full of good soup, a small piece of sausage and, oddly, a small jar of molasses. We untied the benches to seat our guests. Using the upturned Tank for a table again, and sitting on the floor, we had a satisfying meal under the curious stare of all of them. We ate all the soup and half of the noodles, and tucked the bottle of molasses and the sausage into one of the rucksacks.

In the meantime a whole catechism was being fired at us: Where did we come from? Why had we been in prison? Had we been in the black market? (That one with a lot of giggles.) How did we like the Russians? Where were we going? But as they all kept interrupting each other it wasn't hard to give bland and evasive answers and keep the ball rolling till it got out of sight. We were grateful for the food and didn't want to offend the donors, but if we had revealed who we really were, they probably would have felt obliged to hate us. It was better to let them be what they were—simple, kindhearted folk, mis-led by the deceptively simple slogans of a madman and now thoroughly uprooted and anchorless as a consequence of war.

When we had finished our meal, we thanked them all, and one by one they left, Mrs Nut forming the rearguard. We tied the benches together again, but had hardly got our blankets out before she reappeared. This time she wanted to know whom Dries was married to. Quite truthfully, we assured her that we were all bachelors and that the only reason we tied the benches was that they were too narrow by themselves to sleep on, while the floor was too dirty. She would have none of it; she kept popping in and out while we stripped and put on our pyjamas. We stood around for a while, hoping for Mrs Nut to get tired of the game, but she didn't, and we were too weary to outwait her. "All right, Zip," said Dries resignedly, "let's be married for one night, but let's tuck the girls in first."

We made Joke and Nell as comfortable as possible in their narrow wooden cradle, then retired to our own.

"Now I know," Mrs Nut cried happily, and retired for the night, slamming the door behind her. We settled down to sleep, comfortable in the knowledge that we had talked the subject over at the beginning of our friendship. None of us girls had menstruated for the last six months; Dries, after the first two nights of cuddling up close for lack of space, had confided that we didn't have to worry because, much as he loved the atmosphere, he couldn't have an erection. We knew that much about each other: our starved bodies would need a longer time of regular feeding before they would respond to sexual impulses again.

Chapter Five

THE next morning I awoke with a sharp pain in my chest. I saw sunlight streaming into the room and found Dries's elbow firmly planted on my chest. I wriggled to get out from under him, but without success. Emaciated as he was, he still seemed extremely heavy, and his elbow felt like a sharpened spike. Supporting one shoulder against the back of my bench, I planted my feet against the back of his bench and pushed with all my might. The string that held the benches together at the bottom broke, the benches slid apart, and the lower halves of both our bodies fell through to the floor.

Dries swore, flailed his arms, and came awake. The noise woke Joke and Nell, and for a while we sat on the narrow benches, flexing our stiff joints, yawning, and trying to straighten out in our minds such basic questions as where we were, why, and what we were supposed to do next. "It must be at least seven-thirty," I said.

Joke leaped up, darted into the lavatory, poked her head back to announce, "It's all ours," and disappeared again. One by one, with the others guarding the various doors against interruptions of our privacy—and twice there was great banging and rattling of knobs—we had a luxurious morning scrub, complete with running water, soap, toothpaste, and a flushing toilet. I brushed by teeth twice because it felt so good.

We breakfasted on the cold noodles left over from the night before and the four squares of cheese we had saved. Our supplies were running low. We had half a tin of lard, a nearly full tin of jam, the jar of molasses, the sausage, and the dried peas. But the doctor's wife brought us coffee again, and for the time being we didn't worry too much about running out of food.

We sat around sipping the steaming coffee and made plans. Joke and Nell were both tired out and needed a rest. Dries and I had bad blisters on our feet, but were otherwise in fairly good shape. We decided that it would be better to split up and work in teams. In twos, we would run less chance of being picked up by the Russians than if all four together roamed the neighbourhood. Nell and Joke would stay close to our temporary home, keep an eye on our belongings, and try to contact somebody from the British POW camp. Dries and I would follow the river upstream and look for a boat. Our reason for going upstream was simple: it was the wrong direction. We reasoned that if the Russians really were intent on keeping us in their zone and collecting us in their camps, they would guard all routes leading to the American lines but wouldn't bother much about those that led away from them. Once we had the boat, of course, we would have to risk going in the right direction, but our whole plan was based on the assumption that very few people would try to go by water and that therefore the river would be relatively unguarded. There was no knowing whether this assumption was right or wrong till we had a boat to test it with. So after a boat we went.

Dries and I got down to the docks unmolested and, from a safe distance, took a good look at the bridge. It was one of those low wooden bridges on pontoons that the Russians can put together in no time, and was about a hundred yards upstream from where the old steel bridge stood wrecked, one of its spans half crushed into the water. There was a fair amount of traffic on the wooden bridge: Russian soldiers in uniform going and coming; liberated Russians in horsecarts and on foot; a group of Czechs with a big flag and a little pushcart crossing over to our side. There were Russian sentries at each end of the bridge, but they didn't seem to take much interest in the traffic. The one at our end spoke briefly to a group of Czechs, then waved them on. We watched all this for a while and also noted with satisfaction that, although the water was nearly up to the highest mark on the dock of the club boat-house, there was still plenty of space under the pontoon bridge for a rowing-boat to pass.

There was no reason for us to cross the bridge, so we set off along a wandering path that led from the club boat-houses into some thickets along the bank. It was a quite pleasant little path of hard-packed earth that wound its way easily around clumps of trees from one grassy patch to another, and it followed the river bank close enough for us to keep looking for any sign of a boat. There was nobody around, and Dries started to spin a yarn about how this had been the lovers' lane of the members of the boat-clubs and how now they didn't dare use it, and there weren't any movies running either, and where the hell could those frustrated lovers go? "Boy," he exulted, "that'll stop the birth-rate for their cannon-fodder!"

At that precise moment a very small Russian soldier with a very big tommy gun popped out of the bushes in front of us and barred our way. He looked so fierce and bristling that I gave up right away and was ready to turn back. But not Dries. In the best of his sign language and all the Russian words we had picked up, appropriate or not, he argued, cajoled, expostulated, beseeched. Watching him, I couldn't help enjoying the show and reflecting that Dries would do very well in amateur theatricals. Maybe if he hadn't been so much bigger, he would have convinced his opponent. But Dries was tall and gaunt; the soldier was short and roly-poly, and he seemed to get a real satisfaction from tripping up this beanstalk.

This time we had no chance but to cross the bridge. We had promised Joke and Nell that we would try upstream only, so that if we disappeared they would know at least in what direction. We hung around for a while till we saw a fairly big group of Russian ex-POWs approaching the bridge. We fell in with them and passed in a breeze, without either of the sentries giving us so much as a glance.

"You never know with these Russkis, do you?" said Dries, when we were safely on the other bank. It was a remark we would make often, for we never learned to predict what a Russian would do. Was he going to shoot? Be friendly? Look the other way? Help us out? Run us into a displaced-persons camp? In the course of our voyage they did all these things —but we never could tell beforehand what it was going to be.

On this side, the river bank was a low, grassy dike with a narrow cinder path on top of it. We set off along this path. On our right was the river Elbe, muddy brown with silvery patches where the sunlight struck running shivers of wavelets. On our left was a great expanse of green pastures, broken here and there by fences and clumps of trees. There were no cattle any-where and the only farm-houses we could see were quite a long way back from the river. Only very occasionally would a grassy path run from a distant farm-house to the river, but we saw not a single jetty or small landing-place that would indicate a boat-owner among the farmers. Our search didn't seem hopeful, yet one thing kept us stumbling along on our blisters: wherever the river made a bend there were two high poles with red-and-white markers at the top, either on our bank or on the opposite one. Coming as we did from a country criss-crossed by rivers and dependent on water traffic, we knew that these poles were navigation markers for river barges. And if there were barges on this river, there must also be rowing-boats and landing-docks and maybe small harbours. With this kind of talk we kept each other's spirits up and our burning feet moving round one bend and then round the next one.

Our sight of the big farm was unexpected. Our eyes had been glued to the river, scanning both banks, and we had come to take the empty grassland to our left for granted. Yet there it was, a big farm built in a great square around a courtyard accessible by a big portal in one side of the square, and the whole only about a hundred yards from the dike, lying below it, so that from where we stood we could look over its brown thatched roofs and into the courtyard. Dries and I took a quick glance at each other, another at the river, and with one movement swung inland and scrambled off the slope of the dike. Even if the farm had no dock and therefore probably no boat, it offered a chance of food and a rest, and we were hungry and tired.

We approached the portal and looked into the courtyard. From the dike we had seen a great shapeless pile in the middle of this yard; we now discovered that this was made up of half-burned furniture, chunks of manure, and bales of straw that had been too tightly packed to burn, but were smouldering here and there. The signs were unmistakable: the Russians had been there. Warily, we entered the yard and looked around us. The three sides of the square seemed to be made up of barns, stables, and other outbuildings. The doors of one barn gaped wide open on emptiness, a trickle of straw leading from the inside to the charred pile. One stable door hung loose and sagging on its top hinge, while the lower hinge, with bits of brick and mortar still attached, clung uselessly to the wood. The fourth side of the square looked like the living quarters for the family. There were windows with some neat and polished panes and a lot of broken ones; there were several doors, one of them open; and there was smoke coming out of one of the two chimneys. I listened for the usual barn-yard sounds—the scraping and mooing and chain-rattling of cattle, the cackling of chickens, the barking of dogs—but an eerie silence hung all around us, and I had a fleeting memory of a long-forgotten childhood story, in which Prince Charming entered the court of the haunted castle.

Again Dries and I exchanged a look and in tacit agreement we walked over to the open door of the living quarters. From this entrance we could see through the open door of a kitchen to our left, and the very first thing we glimpsed was a huge stove with several pots bubbling on it and, shoved to a corner, a big bowl full of potato salad speckled green with chives. Propelled by a sudden, savage, twisting of our stomachs, we burst into the kitchen—then stopped just as suddenly. In the rear of the kitchen stood a long oaken table and behind it, much absorbed in what he was doing, stood an obviously Russian ex-slave labourer. We knew the type very well by now: the shaven head, the high cheekbones, the short bull neck on the broad but underfed body. This one was clad in what had once been the best Sunday suit of a German farmer; it hung far too loosely on him, and it was adorned with a gold watch-chain dangling from one waistcoat pocket to the other. His appearance was ludicrous, but the array on the table in front of him was even more so. It consisted of a toy steam-engine surrounded by heaps of burning wood shavings.

For a few seconds we stood and gaped at each other. Then the surprise on his broad face changed to fury and he barked a stream of terrible sounds at us. Seeing that we did not move, he grabbed a handful of the burning chips and wildly flung them in our direction. We turned and fled, but Dries, with great presence of mind, shot out a long arm and scooped up a handful of potato salad. We turned a corner, sped along a dark corridor, and came to rest half-way up a staircase, where we sat down and contentedly licked the potato salad off Dries's fingers. It tasted heavenly.

The silence around us was uncanny. We crept up the staircase to explore further. The first room we entered was a shambles, with torn bedding trailing over the pieces of a dismantled iron bedstead, a heavy chair lying smashed against a wall, and bits of plaster from walls and ceiling all over the place. The windows evidently had been opened to throw out the furniture, then the small panes broken for good measure. By comparison the second room, a small bedroom, was almost neat. The bedding had been thrown off the bed, the mattress was missing, bits of glass and wood from broken picture-frames were scattered over the floor, but the rest of the furniture and the windows were intact. In the third and largest bedroom we found a youngish blond woman, cowering against a bed with two small children. The room had not been disturbed; the two beds were piled high with bulky, typically German eiderdowns. If it were not for the eiderdowns, I might have felt some pity. But for three months, in Waldheim, we had been forced to tear goose feathers apart to make those self-same eiderdowns—there was no pity in my heart.

We did not exchange a word. They stared at us, we stared at them; then we turned, closed the door, and went back down the stairs.

Avoiding the kitchen, we found a parlour that had been totally wrecked, window panes and all, then a ladder leading down to a cellar. There wasn't much light in the cellar, but enough filtered down through a small latticed opening at ground level to point out two bins brimful of potatoes and another one half full of turnips. We lost no time in stuffing our pockets and were debating whether Dries would take his shirt off, so that we could carry more potatoes in it, when we were interrupted by a terrific outburst of howls and shouts from above. "Come on," I urged, "we'd better get out of here."

We climbed the ladder fast, rushed through the corridor, then hesitated as we had to pass the open kitchen door. It was now abundantly clear that all the noise emanated from there.

While we stood clutching each other, uncertain whether to make a dash for it or to retreat into the shadow till the fracas was over, a hollering Russian soldier danced out of the kitchen door, saw us, grabbed us, and dragged us into the kitchen. Frightened as I was, I burst out laughing the second I realised what was going on: our furious friend in the Sunday suit had succeeded in making the steam-engine work! There it was, turning its wheel, giving off ridiculous little puffs of steam and shrill whistles. Our friend was jumping up and down behind the table, clapping his hands above his head. Dancing and shouting around the kitchen, hugging each other and hollering, were five more Russians—two young soldiers in uniform and three other ex-prisoners in stolen civilian clothing. Willy-nilly we were drawn into this Indian war dance; for a while we jumped and shouted and applauded with the best of them, laughing till the tears stood in our eyes.

Finally I managed to draw one of the soldiers near to the stove and, still shouting, pointed to the food. He understood, laughed happily, and started bringing the pots to the table. From a rack behind the sink Dries and I grabbed some plates and spoons; soon we were all standing around the table (there was only one chair that had not been thrown onto the pile in the yard, and by rights that belonged to Sunday Suit) and stuffing ourselves. There was soup, there were two pots of stew, and there was the potato salad. The middle of the table, where all the burning chips had been piled up, had taken fire and was smouldering along slowly. The steam-engine was still merrily blowing away, and every once in a while one of the Russians would point to it, throw his head back and roar. In answer we would bang our spoons on the table and shout; then one of the ex-prisoners, who was eating from the upturned lid of a pan, would bang the lid back on the pan, scattering stew all over the place, fill it up again, and continue singing. It was an extremely happy meal.

When we felt we couldn't eat another mouthful and the steam-engine was running out of power, the whistle coming less rapidly now and sounding more melancholy, we put down our plates and started around the table, clapping every man on the back, pumping their hands and saying "*Spasibo, spasibo*" over and over again. Then we walked out through the court with its ugly-looking pile, through the portal, up the grassy slope, and off along the dike again.

The bright sunlight, reflected from the river, made us squint as we walked along without talking, trying to digest the heavy meal and the jumble of impressions. One thing suddenly popped up in the confusion of my mind and I wondered out loud: "How could it have been so silent at first, if there were six of them there, and the woman with the kids upstairs? I could have sworn the whole place was deserted when we first walked in."

"They were probably asleep somewhere in the hay, and the woman and kids were too scared to make a sound," said Dries. "Anyway, there always is silence around a place where violence has been done. Don't you remember how it used to be in the Jewish parts of Amsterdam after a German raid? You'd go in there trying to find somebody, trying to help, and the streets would be so empty you could hear the echo of your footsteps against the walls. And the houses would all look dead and empty, yet there were still plenty of people there, hiding, watching, silent. . . ."

I remembered, all right, and it seemed strange to be alive and walking along a river in the warm sunshine, with the satisfactory feeling of a heavy meal in my stomach. How many had died? How many Jews? How many resistance workers? How many innocent people caught in a squeeze? How many soldiers?

Dries said, "I wish the hell I could talk Russian. I could've helped that guy with his steam-engine if I'd known how to say so. And I bet they'd have helped us find a boat, they were such a friendly bunch."

"It's funny how quickly they change. One moment they're cruel and savage and stupid, and the next they're generous and kind as can be."

"You mean the raping and the looting and the pillaging? I guess every conquering army behaves like that. It must be such a tremendous relief to a soldier to know that he's out of danger and that his side had won. Do you think the village maidens would be safe if the conquerors happened to be Dutch soldiers?"

I laughed and said, "No, but these fellows are so—I don't know—so childish. Even at their most brutal they're kind of mindless, like little kids.'

We talked some more along these lines; then our attention

switched to what looked like a small beach ahead. There were some trees growing right up to the dike, partly blocking our view, but when we drew near we saw there was a dirt road leading up to the river, a small tavern that had been hidden by the trees, and a small sandy stretch along the river that might very well be a ferrying-place. There were even a half-submerged jetty and a couple of poles sticking out of the water —promising enough, except that there was no sign of either ferry or rowing-boat.

"Look," said Dries, "you go into that tavern and find out if they have any boats, if they do any ferrying, or who does. I'll stay right here and keep watch, and if any boat comes around that bend or from the opposite bank, by God, I'll get it."

I looked around. The opposite bank might have a cross-road or it might not; there were too many trees there to be sure about it. There might even be a boat hidden under one of those overhanging willow-trees, but if there were, we couldn't see it. A bit upstream from where we stood, the river made a sharp bend and was lost from view—no telling what might be around the bend.

"Why don't you go in and I'll keep watch?" I said.

He looked scornful. "What are you going to do when you see a boat making loose from the other side?" he asked.

"I don't know. What would you do?"

"Just leave it to me. I'll get it somehow!"

I reflected on his histrionic power and decided that if it was a matter of simulating a call of distress, he'd probably do better than I could, so, reluctantly, I turned to the tavern while he slid down to the little beach.

The tavern, on close inspection, looked pretty shabby. Peering through a window, I could make out what looked like a small restaurant. I saw about seven tables, all empty. It was very dark inside because, of the four narrow windows, the two that faced the river were shuttered. The only way I could see anything was by putting my face against the window and shutting out the daylight with my hands. That still left a dark space to my right, where the door was. Cautiously I went up to the door and tried it. To my surprise it opened. Facing me at right angles was a long tap-bar, the beer-taps gleaming faintly in the gloom. Damn it, I thought, this *must* be a ferrying-place. This is where the customers come in for a quick one while waiting for the boat.

On the bar, at the end nearest to the door, was one of those bells you hit to get service. I stood next to it and listened intently. There were boards creaking upstairs, rustlings behind the wall of the bar. There were people in this house all right. I hit the bell and the sound startled me, sending me back to the door in a hurry. Once there, with the door wedged safely open, I stood my ground and waited. Nothing happened. Nobody appeared. The doors leading out of the restaurant and the tap-room remained closed. The gloom seemed heavier. I waited some more, then went out quietly, leaving the door ajar, and walked round to the back of the house. A neat little vegetable garden, fenced in with chicken wire and securely closed with a padlocked wooden gate. Two windows and a back door downstairs, three small windows upstairs, all neatly curtained. No panes broken, no burning piles of furniture. Evidently this place hadn't been sacked. Did that mean the Russians hadn't yet been here, that the movements I had heard inside were those of the German owners, holding out on me?

I was getting angry. I jumped over the chicken wire, took a look at the tomato patch in which I landed, decided regretfully that I was too sated to eat any, and went to try the back door. It was locked, and it stayed locked in spite of my hammering and kicking. So did the downstairs windows; yet when I looked up during one waiting period it seemed to me I saw a movement behind one of the upstairs curtains. Changing tactics, I returned to the tomato patch, chose a good ripe fruit, and aimed it carefully for one of the upstairs windows. It made a beautiful splash right in the middle of the left pane, but brought no reaction. Neither did four more tomatoes on the remaining windows.

My whole damned-up, frustrated fury at the Nazis broke loose inside me. Who the hell did these Huns think they were, anyway? Didn't they know they'd been beaten, that they'd better be civil to their conquerors, their victims, and everybody else? For a few furious seconds I considered wrecking their damned vegetable garden; but I couldn't do it. All my life I have loved growing things; during my high-school years I had a small vegetable patch outside town, which I tended with love and wonder, not minding the long bicycle rides back and forth. At that moment I would gladly have murdered a living German with my bare hands, but it was beyond me to hurt these healthy, well-cared-for rows of vegetables. So all I could do was kick the padlocked gate a few times, hurting my toes but succeeding in getting the lower hinge undone, and go back to the front.

The tavern door was ajar, as I had left it. This time I burst in without caution, determined to get through one of those inner doors and tell the Huns inside a thing or two. But when I was half-way along the bar a sudden realisation slowed me down: there were people in the room. I looked around, dazed, and saw two Russian officers sitting quietly at one of the tables in the restaurant. I couldn't see their faces, but their shoulder-blades looked very convincing. Then I became aware of a sullen, heavy-set face watching me from behind the bar. The unmistakably German barmaid had materialised from nowhere! From the corner of my eye I measured the distance to the door. It wasn't too far, shorter at least than from the door to the Russian table, or from them to me. In an ordinary state of mind, I would have beat it then and there. But I was too furious, too exasperated to admit defeat. In a gruff tone I asked, "When is the next ferry?"

"No ferries," she said. It was impossible to read any expression on her face. She could have been watching me from the back windows, or she could never have seen me before. Behind me, I heard the Russians talking quietly to each other. No alarm from that quarter.

This time I tried to put a Russian accent into my German when I asked, "where do you keep the boats?"

"No boats," she said. Still no facial expression.

"What happened to the ferry-boat?"

"There is no ferry-boat."

I knew I was licked. No cajoling would work on this woman, and I had no threats at my disposal. Drawing myself up as straight as I could, I sneered, "No boats, eh? Well, no business either," and walked out. It wasn't till I had reached the beach that I realised nothing had happened. She hadn't called out after me, she hadn't screamed for the Russians to go after me, and the Russians themselves had paid no attention to me at all.

But I had no time to mull things over, for right there in the water in front of me were four small boys playing with a boat, and right here at my feet, stretched out full length upon the sand and sound asleep, was Dries. All my fury broke from me, unchecked by fear or frustration. Viciously I kicked him, in the ribs, in the buttocks, in the shins, while he scrambled to get up and out of my way. And then he was standing there, a few feet away, sleep and surprise and hurt in his blue eyes.

"Zip!" he shouted, "Zippie, what the matter, Zippie, for Christ's sake!"

"You big lug!" I screamed, "you were going to keep watch, you let me walk into that trap, there's a boat, you idiot, and you let me go in there alone, and you're asleep, and there's a boat and you are slee-ee-eeping."

I found myself sobbing and crying in Dries's arms and I heard his anxious voice over my head, saying: "Zippie, what happened? What trap? Are you hurt? That boat's no good. It leaks and it only has a paddle. What happened, Zippie? They came around the bend just after you left, and I knew the boat was no good. I could just as well wait till you came back—they couldn't go far. I'm sorry I fell asleep. Zippie, what did they do to you? Did I let you down?"

I felt ashamed of myself, yet thoroughly relieved. We sat close to each other on the little beach and I told him what had

H

happened. It sounded so silly that at the end of my tale we were both laughing. We returned to the business at hand. I agreed that the boat the boys were playing with would be of no help to us. It was one of those flat-bottomed, flimsy things that farmers use to transport hay from one side of a river to the other—a small one at that—and, as Dries had said, there were no oars, only a paddle.

We looked at the sun and decided we had time to explore around the next bend, and if we found nothing there we would have to turn back in order to cross the Russian bridge before sunset. We knew enough about the Russians by now to realise that to them sunset was curfew, no matter what the official orders said.

It was the best decision we ever made. The bend was only a few hundred yards from the crossroads where we had been sitting. As soon as we rounded it we saw an incredible sight: two big river barges tied up at the opposite bank, both flying a Dutch flag, a real honest-to-goodness Dutch flag—three horizontal stripes, red, white, and blue! None of this vertical business that was French, none of this triangular business that was Czech. We yelled and hollered, but not for long. It was quite obvious that whoever was aboard wouldn't react to yells, even if they could hear them against the wind. We had to do better. Dries had the right idea: "Come on," he shouted. "The boys' boat!" We raced back round the bend; Dries ran right into the water and did a beautiful job of commandeering the boat from the surprised boys. I paused long enough at the edge of the water to remove my shoes and roll up my slacks; then I waded in after him, and together we carefully pushed the little nutshell around the bend and far enough upstream so that a bit of steering and paddling would land us right on top of the barges —or so we thought. But we did not know how strong and tricky the current was in the middle of the river, or how weak we were ourselves. The simple feat of pulling the boat upstream for about a quarter of a mile had exhausted us, and instead of stopping and resting we boarded our craft at once and set off.

Before we were even half-way, it was evident that we could not cope with the current and would be swept far below the barges, probably round the bend, and might never make the other side at all. We started yelling again, but this time in an organised way. First Dries would give off with something like "Hey, Hollanders!" Then I would try something like it. Then we would sing the first line of our national anthem together. This brought results. A blond head appeared from the wheelhouse of the first barge, a brown one from the next. We doubled the volume of our shouts—and—oh, bless them—in no time at all Blond and Brown were rowing towards us in a sturdy dinghy. They met us about half-way and expertly brought us to the barges against the current, exchanging information all the way.

"You Dutch?"

"Yes, are both these barges Dutch?"

"Yes, we're all of us Hollanders, where're you from?"

"We come from a prison in Waldheim and we're trying to go home. How do you come to be here?"

"Bridges are all down, we can't move. Where's Waldheim?"

"About thirty miles due south from here."

"Well, come aboard."

They had brought us to the barge nearest the bank, where the water was shallow and full of reeds. A ladder hung from the barge and at the top of it a tall blond skipper stood waiting. In my excitement I committed the unpardonable sin of stepping on the gunwale of our frail boat, which already had shipped considerable water. It promptly sank under me as I grabbed the ladder and got my foot on a rung. The two boys in the dinghy laughed mightily and retrieved it with perfect ease, turning it upside down over the prow of their rowing-boat. Dries and I managed to climb the ladder and stood face to face with the tall blond giant we had seen from below. He stuck out a huge paw and said, "My name is Hartmans. Welcome to Dutch soil."

It was too much for both Dries and me. *"Hollandse grond"*

(Dutch soil)—it was the kind of music that strikes directly to the soul, and our souls had been starved for that music for so long that they were utterly defenceless.

Next thing we knew, we were sitting in the cosy little kitchen with Asmus the other skipper, his wife, his son (the blond one), and Hartmans and the brown-haired boy who was his son. They told us their story. They had been Rhine skippers and the Germans had forced them to come over to the Elbe. Hartmans's barge, the *Damco 35*, was owned by an inland shipping company which had given in to German pressure and told Hartmans to make the move. Asmus's case was a little different. He worked for a big company too, but he owned his own barge, the *Codam 85*, and had held out against all kinds of pressure till the middle of 1944. But he and his family had to live, and when the fighting around the Rhine made the usual shipping routes impossible, they finally had come over to the Elbe too. Now both barges were stuck between battered bridges. The Hartmanses could abandon their barge, if they wished, to make their way home like all other ex-slave labourers. But Asmus's whole working capital and his life's savings were tied up in the barge and he was determined to stick with it.

However, at this time neither of the skippers had any thought of returning to Holland. There was no sign of any rift between the Russians and their Western Allies, and the skippers were simply waiting for the rubble of the bombed bridges to be cleared away and the pontoon bridges to be replaced, so that they could go home in their barges. Skippers are resourceful people; these two, when they saw the collapse of Germany coming, had tied up together in a good spot. Across the river, they told us, was a small village where they could get milk and eggs. On their side, a few miles away, there had been a German airfield plus barracks. When the troops scattered, the skippers hadn't waited for an army from either side to move in; they had simply moved in themselves with a few organised mules and removed all the stores. This explained the raisin cake and tea that we were eating, and the cigarettes that we were now offered. As we didn't have any left ourselves, we accepted them with alacrity. The skippers laughed and told us how they had liberated an abandoned barn full of cured tobacco-leaves, and to help ourselves. The two young boys, Oscar and Kees, started quietly rolling cigarettes for us so that we could take them with us. Somehow they had organised real cigarette paper, too!

Dries and I were completely overwhelmed. The first greeting had thrown us off balance and we had not quite recovered. The whole atmosphere of the little kitchen was so thoroughly Dutch, from the shape of the stove to the big teapot, from the caned chairs and flowered table-cloth to the simple honesty of the people we were dealing with, that we would choke up in the middle of a sentence and helplessly look at each other, hoping that the other one would keep up the hard-faced matter-of-factness that had been so far our defence against the world. Neither of us could make it. But we did eventually tell our story—at least the most important part: that Nell and Joke were waiting for us in Riesa and that we had set out to find a boat in order to go home.

At this point both skippers set up a great roar, calling each other names and laughing with great gusto. It turned out that this was the best thing we could have said. A party of three barge-hands had set off from this very spot on the same mission, and another party of three had passed two days before, also barge-hands and skippers' sons coming from barges farther upstream. We had proved our true Dutch blood to the skippers and they needed no more. "Come back here tomorrow," they said, "and we'll have a boat for you. There's a German barge upstream that has two rowing-boats. We'll organise one of them for you. You'll need supplies for at least three days. We'll supply you, and we can give you a lot of tobacco-leaves; that's better than money." Skipper Asmus and his wife had another thought after their neighbours had left: "If those two girls you're talking about look as bad as you two, you'd better stay over here a couple of days and let us feed you. Why don't

you stay over for Whitsun [May 21st and 22nd] and we'll put
you kids back into shape?"

Quite honestly, we told them that it was up to Nell and Joke,
but that we would be back the next day anyway to get the
boat. There was some discussion of getting the boat now, but
we couldn't think of any way of safeguarding it during the
night, and the final decision was that we would return the next
day, all four of us with our meagre belongings.

It was time for Dries and me to leave. The skippers told us
that we were about six miles upstream from Riesa (all we had
been able to do in half a day) and we knew no better way of
getting back than on our own sore feet. But skipper Asmus had
a much better idea. "You can go back in that cockleshell you
came in," he declared. "I bet the boys are fixing it up right
now." Sure enough, when he called out, "Oscar! Kees!" the
answer came from way below the high-riding, empty barge.
We peeked over the side and the two boys grinned up at us
from their dinghy. They were holding our hay-mover next to
them, with some fresh black patches on its bottom. After we
had clambered down the ladder and gingerly taken place in our
conveyance, they explained that they had put tar over the
leaks, and we would be perfectly safe till we reached Riesa.
Then they handed us the cigarettes they had rolled for us, at
least twenty each, and with their rowing-boat nudged us into
the current. From there on we floated back, Dries nonchalantly
steering with the paddle and both of us smoking to our hearts'
desire. We felt like kings.

Landing gave us no difficulty. Dries just steered out of the
stream at the right moment and our hay-mover, about half-full
of water in spite of the efforts of the barge-boys, settled with
a quiet *gglluugg* on the beach in front of the club-house. Dusk
was falling and the streets were empty. Dries and I walked
back to the doctor's house without any interference. We were
both in a mood of relaxed optimism and considerable self-
satisfaction. We had done what we set out to do and came
home expecting to be praised. But the atmosphere in the

waiting-room was not propitious. Joke looked downright dejected and Nell had that belligerent look on her face which
meant that she had thought up a scheme and that we had better
pay attention.

We tacitly decided to let them talk first and they told the
following story: They had met a Captain Barker who belonged
to the British POW camp and who had just returned from Leip-
zig, where he had made arrangements with the Americans for
evacuation of the Tommies, the first fifteen hundred of whom
would leave by truck the next morning for a place called
Plauen. From there they would be flown home in American
transport planes. Captain Barker was expecting a Red Cross
officer the next day and had written down the names and par-
ticulars of our three patients in Waldheim, with the promise to
give them to the Red Cross officer and also to mail them to the
Red Cross in Holland as soon as he himself got back to England. Naturally the girls had made a request for us to be flown
out too, but had been politely and firmly turned down. As a
consolation, however, the Tommies had given them two and a
half loaves of bread—a very welcome addition to our dwind-
ling food supply.

Dries and I elicited all this information before we discovered
the reason for their downcast mood. After their successful discussion with the British, the girls had decided to take a little turn
around the town, to find out the general atmosphere and grapevine gossip. The news had not been good; they had personally
seen a small group of Frenchmen being marched off in the
direction of the bridge and the displaced persons camp, called
Zeithain, that lay across it. They were being guarded by a
Russian soldier with the inevitable tommy gun. Joke had
shouted in French, "What happened to you?" and they had
answered, "They picked us up—we have to go to the camp."
Whereupon both girls had had to flee around a corner, for the
soldier had noticed them and was making motions for them to
fall in and follow the little column.

Soon after, they had heard that dreadful word "passes"

again. Everybody needed passes. Two Czech ex-prisoners they met on the street had proudly exhibited theirs—yellow slips of cardboard with some Russian words printed on them—and had given directions to the office of the Russian Kommandant where passes could be obtained. As Joke and Nell well knew, it was quite a different matter for Czechs, Poles, and Yugoslavs to obtain these necessities of life than it was for us. Their languages were all Slavic and they always managed to understand the Russians and vice versa. Even more important, they didn't have to cross the Russian lines to get back to their countries, which had been our greatest stumbling-block from the start. On their way to the square where the Kommandant's office was located, the two girls met several more little groups of former prisoners and slave labourers, recognisable as always by the small flags sewn on their clothes and their underfed, unkempt look. Some of them had passes, most of them did not, and none of those who had passes were Westerners.

Once they arrived at the square the office wasn't hard to find; an unruly, multilingual, ragged mob was shoving and pushing in front of what looked like a theatre-ticket window in the wall of an office building marked by a Red Army flag. It had taken the girls more than an hour to worm their way through, each working from a different direction. Nell got to the window first and Joke was close on her left, but they had hardly started to explain their mission when a resounding *"Nyet"* was spat in their faces and the window was slammed down. The Russians were through for the day.

They had made their way back to the doctor's house as fast as they could and had sat there waiting for us, fearing we had been caught and marched off to the camp like the Frenchmen. "And now," said Nell, setting her jaw, "I really think we ought to change plans. Even if we get a boat——" "We have one," interjected Dries, but Nell wasn't ready to listen. "We obviously will need a pass, and they aren't giving any to Westerners. The point is that eventually everybody hanging around here is going to be picked up and put into a camp forcibly.

Now suppose we go there of our own free will? We'll get there first and have priority when they start moving us. Who knows, those who come voluntarily may be moved directly west—it seems so damn' impractical, even for Russians, to move everybody to Odessa first. I think we should simply go to the camp tomorrow and take all our stuff with us."

"I just don't know what to do," said Joke despairingly.

"Wait till you hear our story," said Dries. While he launched into it backwards with the jubilant statement, "I tell you we have got a boat!" and then proceeded to fill in all the details, I sat watching Nell and Joke. Nell, although as good a resistance member as any, was basically a law-abiding person; when the odds were against us, she believed it was the better part of wisdom to obey. Joke, young and child-like though she was, had shown incredible courage in guiding shot-down Allied pilots over the Dutch-Belgian border on the first leg of their arduous journey back to freedom. In prison she had often acted with great self-sacrifice. I had always had an un-disciplined nature, and although I often agreed with Nell that obedience would keep us out of trouble, I was even more con-vinced that disobedience, resistance, and sheer cussedness were good for the soul, especially for a soul in captivity. When-ever the three of us had shared a cell in the long line of prisons we had been through, and I had cooked up some new scheme for contacting other prisoners, for getting news in and out of the jail or for merely annoying the guards, we had had this same argument, and it had usually been Joke who gave the de-ciding vote, siding either with me or with Nell. Now, watching them, I knew it wouldn't take long to convince Joke. Her eyes sparkled as soon as she heard about the Dutch barges, and she soon fired to Dries's glowing tale. It took somewhat longer with Nell, but among the three of us we had little trouble overcom-ing her last objections and, good scout that she was, she plunged into a discussion of our next moves with as much enthusiasm as any of us.

It was quite a happy evening, Mrs Nut waddled in again

with a pan of noodles-and-cheese, and later with a dish of rhubarb for dessert. The doctor himself visited us, too. He looked tired and drawn. He had been busy since dawn at the hospital, which was mostly filled with wounded soldiers but where enough emaciated, sick, or tortured ex-prisoners from a near-by concentration camp had been brought in during the last two weeks to shock him profoundly. We thanked him for his hospitality and told him we would be off early the next morning. As he shook my hand he said, "There are many things we Germans have done to you people that we will never be able to make up for." It left me uneasy. I remembered what I had said to Joke about the red-haired woman and her daughters, and we had seen enough evidence of kindliness among the Germans we had met since our liberation to convince me that not all of them were as bad as the strutting military, the cruel Gestapo, and the brutal prison guards who had ruled us during the five years of Holland's occupation. Yet it was hard for me to consider any one German anything but an enemy.

While we were tying our benches together for the night, Mrs Nut returned once more, this time with a Tommy in tow. It turned out that one of her daughters had befriended this Tommy—no doubt as a "protector" for the family—and that he was among the first batch to be evacuated the next day and had come to say good-bye. I asked him if he would take a letter to my family and mail it when he arrived in England. He agreed, and I sat down to scribble a hasty note to my mother, telling her that I was alive and on my way but didn't know how long it would take, and giving her the addresses of the other three families for relaying the same message. It is a very peculiar feeling to write to your mother, when you do not know whether she—or any other member of your family—is alive or dead, but I got it done; the Tommy promised on his word of honour to mail it.

The next morning Nell and Dries made a second trip to the Kommandant's office and arrived there early enough to be among the first at the window. Behind it sat a young, sullen

Russian girl who spoke a smattering of German. She wasn't impressed with our plan and kept saying, "Nix boat, nix bridge, go to Zeithain camp," but finally gave them a little white slip of paper with some Russian words written on it and a big rubber stamp. Dries and Nell returned with this, quite proudly, although they had no idea of what their piece of paper said. For all we knew, it could simply be a pass to Zeithain and nothing more.

Joke and I having, in the meantime, packed the Pram and the Tank, the four of us set off towards the river. Soon our confidence in our "pass" was greatly reinforced. We had taken the little path that started behind the club boat-houses, the same one where Dries and I had been stopped the day before. At almost the same point we were challenged by another soldier, but when we showed him the slip of paper, he motioned us on! The rest of the hike was uneventful. We swore at our blisters and coaxed the little wagons along the narrow trail, but we had no further encounters or adventures. The approximately six miles to the barges took us two hours, which for us was pretty good going.

We got a reception I will never forget in my life. Skippers Hartmans and Asmus, Mrs Asmus and the two boys, Oscar and Kees, were waiting for us as if we were their own long-lost daughters and son. Again we were installed in the cosy kitchen; this time they produced with a flourish a full bottle of schnapps, and poured us each a glassful. Even before any of us had got caught by the Gestapo, any kind of liquor had been extremely hard to get in Holland. Your prewar dealer might manage to get you a bottle every three months or so; the waiter in your favourite bistro might pour you a glass now and then; but that was the long and the short of it. Yet here were these skippers producing a full bottle at the very end of the war! They laughed at our incredulity and told us that at the near-by airfield they had not only liberated case upon case of German schnapps, but also many gallons of straight alcohol, with which they fabricated their own brand.

Except for the bottle of wine we had found the first night of
our freedom, we had had no alcohol for more than a year, and
as we sat there, sipping the fiery stuff cautiously, we could feel
the relaxation of it seeping through our bodies. The skippers
had no trouble whatsoever in persuading us that it would be
better to stay with them that day and to leave the next morning. At this point Mother Asmus, who until then had been busy
at the stove, announced that the midday dinner was ready—
and what a dinner it was! We had tomato soup, roast veal with
spinach, potatoes and gravy, and rice with raisins for dessert.
Up to this day I am convinced that not many people in occupied or recently liberated Europe ate as well on that particular
Whit-Monday as we did.

Yet, though food was still an enormously important factor in
our starved lives, the warmth, the friendship, and the helpful-
ness of these skipper folk were even more important. We had
been self-reliant outlaws for too long; the relief of being taken
into a warm Dutch family, where we were treated with love
and respect and utter kindness, was almost overpowering. We
talked our hearts out, often all of us at once. We told about the
long, lonely hours of solitary, the filth of the overcrowded cells,
the despair of impotence when cellmates were dying, the small
triumphs whenever we had managed to fool the guards, the
shattering fear when bombs were falling all around and there
was no way of escaping from a locked cell on the top floor of a
prison. It all came out in an incoherent jumble, but somehow
they managed to understand.

There were many other things in that long glorious afternoon. They showed us through the two barges, and we marvelled at their sparkling neatness. Rhine barges are all built
the same way, enormously long, with vertical living quarters:
on top the wheelhouse, next the kitchen, which is even with
the deck and has a door and windows to the outside; underneath that a little-used parlour with portholes, and underneath
that, connected with vertical ladders, from one to three bedrooms with built-in bunks. The Hartmans's boat, though

manned only by father and son, was just as shiningly clean as
the Asmus boat, where a woman was aboard. It was a joy to
see.

We also inspected our boat, a sturdy iron-bottomed rowing-
boat with three oars (one for steering, for it had no rudder)
which the two boys were fitting out for us. They had already
scrubbed it clean, oiled the rowlocks, attached a chain with a
lock to one bench and a length of rope to the other, stuffed a
tarpaulin under the back seat and installed an enormous ten-
gallon demijohn with drinking-water in front of the tarpaulin.
Now, under our eyes, they filled a cardboard box with gro-
ceries: several loaves of bread, six pound tins of meat, bags of
rice and sugar, a box of dried raisins, and a big tightly packed
bag of tobacco-leaves. To this we added our own few supplies;
then everything, including our rucksacks with the blankets and
towels, and last but not least the Pram and the Tank were
securely stowed away or lashed onto the boat. It certainly was
shipshape. When the boys asked us if we wanted to give the
boat a name, we promptly christened it *Montgomery*, and with
glee they painted the name in neat white letters on the
gunwale.

Towards milking time, Dries and I accompanied skipper
Asmus across the river on a quest for milk and eggs. This Asmus
was a first-class organiser. He knew exactly in which four farms
around the village the Russians had herded together all the
cattle of the neighbourhood (which explained why Dries and I
had seen no cattle in the fields), at what time they milked, and
which Russians were most approachable. One day he would go
to one farm, the next one to the next and so on, so that he never
seemed too demanding or too greedy at any one place. He also
told us that the officer in charge in the village had managed to
stop his men looting and raping—by typically Russian methods.
Asmus himself had been present in the village square when an
officer made two of his men kneel on the pavement and killed
them each with a shot in the neck. According to the astonished
villagers, the two had been involved in a rape orgy.

For a while we hung around a big stable and watched the milkers, most of them Germans but a few of them Russian women, and the two Russian NCOs who kept a sharp eye on the collection of the milk. Because the cows were packed tightly in the stable the milkers had trouble wriggling their bodies in between them and had to be careful not to get themselves or their pails stepped on. More cows were tied up outside. Obviously the Russians had decided that, in spite of these inconveniences, it was better to have all the milk at a few central places than to collect it from farm to farm with much less control.

Asmus exchanged a few words of his own brand of Russian with one of the NCOs, who smiled at him and at us and generously allowed us to fill our pail with foaming milk from one of the big collection cans. Then we followed Asmus to the far end of the stable, where we waited till a tall, haggard-looking woman had extricated herself and her pail from between two cows. This was the moment Dries and I had really come for; we wanted a translation of the few words on the slip of paper from the Kommandatura, and this was where Asmus thought we might get it. With his back to the NCO, he showed the woman a small bottle of schnapps he had brought along in his pocket. Her tired black eyes lighted up and she stretched out her free hand. Asmus nudged me, and I mutely put the little paper into the eager hand. She sighed, put down her pail, brushed the damp, straggly hair from her forehead with a dirty forearm and studied the paper. It seemed hours before she said, in halting German, "*Fahren mit schiff, egal wohin*" ("Go with boat, no matter where").

In a flash Asmus handed over the bottle and we were outside, making our way to Asmus's small ferry-boat, Dries and I hugging each other with joy. We almost fell off the ladder in our eagerness to tell Nell and Joke about this utterly unexpected translation of our passport, and when at last we had made it clear to them, all four of us danced with joy on the covers of the hold. If the amused skipper's family hadn't stood laughing along the gangway, catching us every time we skidded from the slightly inclined, slippery boards, one of us would surely have ended up in the river.

As it was, everybody agreed that our good luck called for an appropriate celebration; the bottle of schnapps was brought out again. This time we drank more boldly, and soon we were singing all the songs that had done so much to keep up our morale from one prison to the other. Our own words to familiar songs pleased the skippers. Even though our harmony got progressively worse, we had to sing the more ribald ones over and over again, until Mother Asmus rescued us by turning to the stove and announcing that there would be pancakes in half an hour. This reminded the skippers that it was time to make their rounds, and us that we needed some fresh air.

While we were sitting around after the pancakes, blissfully well-fed and almost overcome with our good fortune, the skippers gave more evidence of their thoughtfulness. They had noticed that Nell's green skirt was badly worn— would she try on these working-trousers and see if they fitted? Nell retired on deck and returned in the well-fitting trousers. Next came a pair of shoes that fitted Joke much better than the poor ones she had been stumbling around in. Nobody on board had shoes my size, but they had found the next best thing: thick woollen socks that would take up some of the space between my raw skin and the hard, chafing leather. To Dries they offered any of the men's clothing he wanted, but Dries answered that he had all he needed to get home in and that their kindness already exceeded anything we could ever repay.

"Don't be silly," said Asmus, and, pointing at Joke, added, "we've got to do something for baby here." Joke spluttered and blushed crimson—she hated any reference to her youth, but the skipper got up, broke an egg into a tumbler, beat it well with a fork and poured schnapps into it. "There," he said, "you need some extra strength." We all laughed at her indignant baby face while Asmus poured a last nightcap for each of us, this time without eggs. Over these he tried once more to persuade us to stay a few days longer. But though life on the barges had been perfectly wonderful, the pull of home was stronger and we were determined to start the next morning. We half climbed, half fell down the steep ladders to the bedrooms and were asleep before we had quite settled into the snug bunks.

A huge breakfast awaited us the next morning, and the skippers had three more presents for us: a bottle of milk, a bottle of alcohol to persuade obstinate Russians, and an alarm clock. Hartmans and his son Oscar decided to accompany us for a stretch to see how things went, and after fond farewells we cast off at exactly 8.20 a.m. by the alarm clock, Hartmans steering us into the current with the extra oar and the rest of us waving at the *Codam 85* and the *Damco 35* till they disappeared behind the bend.

Just before the wooden bridge a bullet pinged into the water in front of us—the Russian sentry's way of summoning us towards him. Hartmans hastily pulled up to where the soldier was lounging in the grass next to the bridge, and he came down to the water's edge and took the slip of paper we confidently held out to him. Here an unexpected hitch developed; he obviously couldn't read! We saw him following the words with a stubby finger, trying to make out the meaning. Then he gave up and returned the paper to us, shaking his head. We pointed to the bridge and to the boat, but he only shook his head again and said, "*Nyet.*" So we got out the bottle of alcohol and passed it up to him for a swig. He grinned happily, took a wide-legged stance, threw back his head and brought the bottle to his lips. Glug-glug-glug-glug. . . . We just sat there, watching in helpless awe while the whole litre of alcohol disappeared down his throat. When the bottle was empty he threw it into the river, nonchalantly waved us on, and fell down on the grass. We cast off and passed under the bridge, mute with admiration, but also realising that we would have to handle any other illiterate sentries without the benefit of alcohol.

At the damaged steel bridge there was no sentry, and we passed unchallenged. Time had come for Hartmans and Oscar to leave us. We put them off, thanked them profusely, and shook their hands. Then I pushed us off with the steering-oar and the boat began to drift with the current. We looked at each other and grinned. We were on the river and on our own. "Go with boat, no matter where!"

Chapter Six

SHORTLY after the Hartmanses left us, the wind turned to the north, slowing our progress considerably. We soon discovered that we couldn't just drift, for the current was tricky, zig-zagging from one bank to the other, and if the current was kind enough to stick to the middle of the river, the wind would push us against the banks. So Dries and I alternated at the oars, not rowing steadily, but enough to keep our *Montgomery* going slowly along in midstream. The sun was shining, the sky stood wide and blue above us, and the river meandered peacefully between grassy banks. Once a couple of Russian soldiers hailed us from the left bank, but all they wanted was to be ferried across, a service we gladly performed. One of them was highly intrigued by our demijohn, but his interest waned when we made it clear that it held water, not alcohol.

Towards noon we came to another pontoon bridge and again the sentry fired to draw our attention, but we knew this trick by now and rowed towards him without undue haste. This one, too, was interested in our demijohn, but by pointing at the bottle and then scooping up some river water and pointing again, we made it clear that there was nothing there for him to get excited about and he let us through without difficulty. Even though this demijohn seemed to attract a lot of Russian attention, we were extremely grateful to the thoughtful skippers who had provided it, for as we manœuvred the boat into position so that we could skip easily under the bridge, we saw two bloated corpses floating among the driftwood that had snagged on the pontoons and were thoroughly glad we didn't have to drink Elbe water.

We had our lunch in the boat, and afterwards took turns lying on the poop, letting our feet dangle in the water. It was absolute bliss not to have to use our feet, and, now that we didn't have to exert ourselves except for some lazy pulls on the oars, we all realized how tired we were. All during the afternoon at least one of us was sound asleep, lying on the poop or curled up in the bottom of the boat.

At 4.30 p.m. Dries, with the aid of his map and the kilometre markers along the bank, had just decided that we must be near the village of Mühlberg when we saw a party of four Russian soldiers standing on the bank to our right. As we drew near, one of them pulled his revolver and shot into the water and they all started to shout. Thinking they wanted to be ferried over, we pulled up to them, but then we discovered that they had other things in mind. They spoke only a few words of German, but with many gestures they made it clear that they wanted our boat and that we should continue on foot with the wagons. Quite naturally, we were violently opposed to this idea and refused to budge. Only one of the four had a revolver and, though he once pulled it out to threaten us, the others restrained him quickly. We came to the conclusion that they were on some personal expedition of their own and had no official right to requisition our boat. Between drawing this conclusion, however, and making them understand that we had seen through their game, there seemed to be an unbridgeable gap. We tried our paper passport, but they said it was no good without the signature of the Kommandant in Mühlberg. Dries, who had just consulted the map, warned us that Mühlberg was at least a mile inland, and that if we consented to go there, the soldiers would have plenty of time to make off with our boat. Next we tried to engage their sympathy. Nell and I happened to be barefoot at that particular time and we showed them our multiple raw blisters, repeating, "*Kaput, kaput,*" indicating that we couldn't possibly walk. This had no effect whatsoever.

The Russian party consisted of two fierce-looking young fellows with decidedly Mongolian features, a man of about thirty-five with a long face and a hawk nose, and a dark-haired, dark-eyed and quite handsome soldier of about twenty-five who, except for his Russian uniform, looked as if he might have come from almost any country in Europe. They talked excitedly among themselves, but we had no idea what they were saying. Dries thought of one other approach: pointing repeatedly at the flags on our clothing, he dug up a pencil and a scrap of paper from a rucksack and started to draw a simplified map that would show the relative geographical positions of Russia and Holland. But the piece of paper was too small for a very clear drawing and Dries was stumped by not knowing what name to write over the tiny spot that was Holland, much less how to write it in Russian characters. Moreover, the Russians weren't interested. Dries was still trying to explain it all with pointing and gestures when one of the Mongolians tore the paper out of his hand, crumpled it disdainfully, and threw it into the river.

Now we reached a stalemate and tried to outwait each other. Both sides gave up any effort at talking. The soldiers sat on the grass, keeping a firm grip on the boat. We sat in the boat and held on to the oars. Dries and I discussed trying to pull the boat away from them, but decided it would be too dangerous. Up to now they had refrained from violence, but their mood was ugly and they might easily be provoked into it if we made a sudden move. After about three-quarters of an hour the soldiers had a new discussion among themselves; as a result two of them, the hawk-nosed one and the Mongolian who had the revolver, got up and left. We breathed a little easier now that the revolver at least was out of the way, but our position was not much improved. The other two remained as firm as ever, except that now they didn't ask directly for the boat but insisted that we go to the Kommandant in Mühlberg.

I sat there, weighing the possibilities in my mind. If all four of us went to Mühlberg, we would lose the boat and everything in it, so that was out of the question. If Dries went alone, we three girls would be left without any manly protection, however feeble, and we would probably all three be raped and maybe lose the boat too. If Joke went—but that was unthinkable. Joke was the youngest among us; she had to be spared at all cost. And Nell? She was weaker than I was and didn't have much experience with men. That left me. The thought was so distasteful that for a while I stopped thinking altogether and just sat and waited again. Dries, trying to appear unconcerned, was humming tunelessly, but I could see the muscles in his jaws working with the rage he was holding back. Nell and Joke were pale and silent. The Russians sat there as if they had all the time in the world. We had been here over an hour now and we would need at least another hour to get far enough away to start looking for safe quarters for the night; from what we had seen along the river so far, they wouldn't be easy to find. That meant we definitely did *not* have all the time in the world.

Suddenly a possible ruse occurred to me. We had heard stories about women who had been raped so often and so roughly that their flesh was all torn, at which point the Russians were no longer interested. Undoubtedly these soldiers knew this too. Anyway, I had to try something; this stalemate could not last for ever. I started putting on my socks and my shoes and said to Dries, "I think I have an idea. I'll pretend I'm going to Mühlberg with one of them, but I don't think he wants to go there himself, so hold the boat ready, I may be back pretty soon."

"Good luck, Zippie," said Dries, his voice strangled with impotent fury.

Getting up, I pointed at the good-looking, dark-haired soldier, pulled our passport from my pocket and, showing it to him but putting it back in my pocket before he could get his hands on it, said imperatively, "Mühlberg. Kommandant!" Then I stepped out of the boat.

A big smile came over his face and he took my hand and led me away quite gently. I threw a quick glance over my shoulder and saw to my satisfaction that the Mongolian had let go of the boat and stood looking after us. For about five minutes we walked silently through the grassy fields, the soldier leading and I following a step behind. We were still holding hands and I didn't try to pull back. This seemed a good way to get his confidence. Then we came to a small hollow, out of sight of the river or the bank. There my handsome companion sat down and patted the grass beside him, inviting me to sit down too. I remained standing, quite close to him, and shook my head sadly. A dark scowl of impatience came over his face and he started tugging at my slacks. This was the moment. Refusing my trembling body the slightest backward movement, I simply shook my head again and, pointing at myself, said softly, "*Kaput.*"

The fellow had an extraordinarily expressive face. In a flash his expression of commanding impatience changed to one of sadness and sorrow. Reaching up, he touched me very gently in the only place that was of importance to him and asked, "*Kaput?*" I nodded, took our passport from my pocket again and held it out to him. With a deep sigh, he produced a stub of pencil and, holding the slip of paper against his knee, laboriously wrote a few words on it. Then he held it up to me and indicated with a move of his head that I could return to the boat. I left him sitting in the grass with his head in his hands, the very picture of dejection.

Now that my ruse had succeeded, my heart was beating in my throat and my legs were trembling. Quickly I scrambled out of the hollow and started to run towards the boat—only to find my way blocked by the Mongolian soldier. I should have thought of this, of course. I knew well enough that the Russians had no objection to taking turns at the same woman; this one had obviously been waiting till his friend was through with me. I had no plan whatsoever for handling this problem and I knew instinctively that showing him his friend's scrawl on our passport would not be of the slightest help. Worse, he might destroy it with the scorn he had shown for Dries's map.

If I had been in a normal state of mind, I would not have

dreamed of tackling him. But I was thoroughly shaken by a mixture of fear and triumph, and the abrupt realisation of new danger made me furious with frustration. I was still running when I came up to him. He grabbed me roughly by one shoulder. I brought my free hand around and pushed his chin up as far as I could. This made him get rougher. He grabbed my other shoulder and drew me up against him so hard that I lost my grip on his chin. Desperately, I brought up my knee sharply between his legs. He grunted in pain and staggered back. I kicked him hard in the same spot and this time he fell into a sitting position. Dodging his wildly grabbing hand, I rushed past him and got to the river bank. Dries was waiting at the oars. I half jumped, half fell into the boat, and Dries pulled away immediately and kept pulling. It was just in time. We weren't even in midstream when the Mongolian, waving his arms and shouting at the top of his lungs, appeared at the bank. Now it was his turn to be furious and frustrated; he even left the bank and waded a few steps into the river. But either the water running into his boots or the slippery mud under his feet must have brought him to his senses, for he turned back and stood on the bank shouting what must have been a fine choice of Russian obscenities at us.

"It's a good thing he isn't the one who has the revolver!" I said from the bottom of my heart.

"Are you all right, Zip?" the others asked anxiously.

"Certainly," I answered. "I haven't been raped, and I've got something new written on the back of our passport, though I don't know what it says. It's just that now I seem to be even more scared than I was when I started out!"

It was true. I was shaking all over. Every fibre of my body, every little recess of my mind, seemed to be cringing from a danger that, after all, was past. Joke tucked a blanket around me and for a while I lay in the bottom of the boat, staring up at the now pale blue and mother-of-pearl sky, trying to get my trembling under control and wondering about this silly way of reacting to danger. The same thing had happened after several

close brushes with border guards or the Gestapo during my
years of resistance, and again, after I was caught, during the
long Gestapo interrogations. While the actual danger was
present, I would be scared all right, but either completely calm
and scheming or so ridiculously foolhardy that my opponents
would be taken aback just long enough for me to escape. But
after it had passed, my fears would get the better of me and I
would be a quivering little coward. Vaguely, I remembered
that my father had told me something about adrenalin, "the
chemical component of courage" as he called it, produced by
the human body under moments of stress. But why couldn't
this adrenalin, which produced cold-headed scheming and
wildcat fighting, last long enough to supersede these fears-
after-the-act? I decided it was probably because I never
planned far enough. As in my chess game, I am able to plan
three of four moves ahead, but no further, because I become so
confused that I prefer to trust to luck—and to foolhardiness, if
need be. I'll have to become a better chess player, I thought
to myself; then, noticing that my trembling had stopped, I sat
up to inquire where we were.

A little way downstream was a small inlet, and anchored
there was a badly listing barge. Dries was pulling towards it,
for the time was nearly eight o'clock and the barge looked like
an ideal shelter for the night. Because of the list, and because we saw no movement aboard, we assumed that it was
abandoned, but when we had made fast and clambered aboard,
we found a German skipper's family living on it. The barge had
been looted and damaged, they told us, and had shipped water
in the deepest part of their living quarters and the adjoining
hold, but the forward hold was empty and dry; if we wanted
to spend the night there, they had no objection. They warned
us, however, that almost every night Russian soldiers from an
encampment in the near-by village of Belgern had come by on
looting and raping expeditions and that both the women on
board had been raped. We debated whether to stay or seek a
safer place downstream, but the odds were that we would find

no roof over our heads at all, and the Red Army was everywhere, anyway.

We took the precaution of unloading all our luggage and bringing the boat around to the river side of the barge, where it could not be seen from the bank. Next we lifted one of the covers from the forward hold and descended into it by way of a wooden ladder we found on deck. The hold was indeed empty, except for a big stack of delicious-smelling pinewood at the far end and a pile of tarpaulins. We dragged the tarpaulins behind the woodstack and, spreading them in such a way that they corrected the list of the barge, arranged a cosy, dark bedroom. The floor of the hold was covered with large steel plates. On one of these, near the opening above us, we collected a pile of wood chips and lit a small fire, over which Nell heated a can of stewed meat and made some real coffee.

After the meal we rolled some cigarettes and while we sat around smoking, I told the others exactly what had happened in the meadows of Mühlberg.

"Pretty smart," commented Dries, "kicking him where it would hurt most."

"I think the *kaput* story is even better," chuckled Joke.

Their praise pleased me greatly, but I had no desire for a repeat performance; before we crawled into our bedroom, I took the ladder away from the opening, deciding that not even our exuberant Russian comrades would risk jumping down into the blackness of the hold. Once during the night we were awakened by shots and screams from the bank, but there was no movement on the barge itself, and we soon fell asleep again, except for Dries, who was struggling with a stomach ache.

We were up early the next morning. The first thing we did was climb up on deck to see if our "Monty" was still safe. It was. After private excursions to some bushes on the bank and a quick wash in the river, we returned to the hold, made another fire, and had bread and hot coffee for breakfast. Then we lugged our belongings back to the boat again, lashed everything safely, and set off a little after eight.

The wind was still against us. For the first hour the sun shone brightly, but then great clouds started piling up overhead, the wind became stronger, and it turned cold. Dries, who still had trouble with his stomach, wrapped himself in a blanket and the tarpaulin and lay down in the bottom of the boat in front of me. Nell curled up behind me. On the poop, half tucked under the wheels of the Pram, lay a ball of blanket, with some frizzly hair sticking out, which was Joke. I was at the oars with our piece of canvas wrapped around me. Quietly I rowed along, glancing over my shoulder now and then to make sure that I followed the bends of the river, resting whenever I felt like it and letting the boat drift till it needed a little steering. I didn't have to worry about bumping into any other boats for the *Montgomery* was manifestly the only boat on the river. The landscape became more varied now; in places the banks were so low that I could see over them toward a farm here and there, farther inland. In other places small woods bordered the river and a lot of birds flew about. Once I held the boat steady for about ten minutes, watching a brilliant kingfisher dart from a low branch into the water, come up with a small fish, swallow it sitting on his perch, and dart down again.

Then, as I rounded a bend and looked over my shoulder to see which direction the river was taking, I noticed another pontoon bridge in the distance. Reaching over, I extricated the alarm clock from behind the demijohn. It was half-past noon and I decided that my companions had slept enough, so I prodded them all awake. As we came nearer we could see buildings reaching down to the river on both sides of the pontoon bridge and a jumble of twisted steel girders sticking up behind it. Dries got out his map and decided that this must be the town of Torgau and its big railway bridge which had been destroyed. The usual bullet came whistling past us as we approached. We made fast at a mooring-ring set in a stone quay, and were somewhat surprised to see a woman officer come out of a wooden sentry box. She was in full uniform, with stars on her shoulders that indicated some kind of rank. As she came striding towards us in her heavy boots, a rifle slung nonchalantly over her shoulder, Joke whispered in awe, "Do you think they had women in the front lines too?"

The woman gave us no trouble. She smiled at the slip of paper we handed to her, passed it back, and motioned that we could go through. But we had hardly emerged at the other side of the bridge, when we were summoned to the quay again, this time by a male officer. Cursing, we rowed over to him, but this time it turned out that he had called us only out of kindness. Gesticulating, pointing to our boat and to us in turn, and repeating the word *"Kaput"* over and over, he made it clear that he didn't think we could get through the ruins of the railway bridge alive. When we looked incredulous, he waved his arms, inviting us to come up and have a look for ourselves. He seemed so excited that we gave in and, leaving Joke and Nell to guard the boat, Dries and I climbed onto the quay and walked with the officer the four hundred yards or so down to the demolished bridge. Then we saw what he meant. The whole steel bridge was down in the water, effectively blocking the river, so that the waters of the wide, deep Elbe had to pour through one narrow gap about four yards wide. As a result our peaceful, broad, slow-moving stream was transformed into a raging, roaring torrent that pushed through the gap at terrific speed and fell at least three feet before it could widen out again to its usual contours. I looked about to see if there was any way of carrying, or more likely dragging, our boat round this obstacle. But the wreckage of twisted steel continued over the quay and between the buildings. Whoever had bombed or blown up this bridge had done a very thorough job. There simply was no passage except by water if we wanted to keep the boat.

I became aware of a spirited conversation going on between Dries and the Russian officer; after listening for a minute, I realised that they were both talking their own languages, with an occasional *"kaput"* (from the officer) and *"nix kaput"* (from Dries) as the only concessions to any lingua franca. "Look," Dries was saying in the purest Dutch, "I'm a seaman, you see,

and I know all about water and——" Then he was interrupted
by a stream of Russian which I could only guess at. "But you
don't understand," Dries resumed, "we were brought up in a
country of sea and rivers. Why, half our country consists of
water and we know how to handle it and how to steer our
boats on it." More Russian. And so on. They were walking back
towards the "Monty" now and I trailed behind them, marvel-
ling at this conversation and at the mysterious ways that men
have of understanding one another. I knew, of course, that
Dries was bluffing. Holland has plenty of water all right, but
the country is so flat that the water moves sluggishly, and
electric pumps are often needed to speed it on its way to the
sea. Rapids are unknown in Holland; I was pretty sure that
Dries, even during his years as a merchant seaman, had never
come up against a situation like the one that faced us now. I
felt very grateful to this Russian for showing us the danger, for
from our low boat we would not have noticed it until we were
too close, and then, in all likelihood, the whirlpools of angry
water would have sucked us against the wreckage of the bridge
and tossed us around until we were thrown into the gap, probably at the wrong angle. I remembered a book I had read as a
teen-ager about Lewis and Clark travelling swift rivers in the
American Northwest, and reflected that that was almost all I
knew about rapids. I tried to recall what the theory was about
the approach to rapids, by my memory was confused. I con-
soled myself with the thought that they had had light canoes
where we had a clumsy, heavy rowing-boat, so their theories
wouldn't apply anyway.

We had arrived back at the mooring-ring where the *Montgomery* was tied up, and Dries and the officer were saying fond
good-byes to each other. I joined them, held out my hand to the
Russian, said a heartfelt *"Spasibo"* and, with a side-glance at
Dries, added *"Nix kaput!"* He roared at that and gave me an
iron-handed slap on the shoulder. But once we were all back in
the boat, I said to Dries, "Okay, Admiral, what do we do
next?"

Dries was not to be shaken. He was every inch the captain, asking brisk questions and giving brief commands. "You stood looking at that fall for quite some time," he said to me. "Did you see any pieces of the bridge or any rocks showing among the foam?"

"No," I answered, "I didn't, and if there were any, I think that by now they would probably have been pushed farther downstream. That water carries a terrific punch."

"So I thought," he said. "Now I'll tell you what to do. Nell and Joke, you lie low in the boat and hang on to everything that's loose. We may be tossed about quite a bit and we may ship some water, but you stay where you are till I tell you we're through. Joke, be sure to protect our drinking-water. Nell, be sure not to pop up and obstruct our view. Now, Zip, I want you to take the steering oar. Go sit on the poop and steer me so we are in a straight line with the gap. Do you remember where it is?"

I nodded. Almost unconsciously, during our excursion, I had fixed in my mind a picture of the exact formation of the twisted steel on both sides of the gap. The training of the resistance came in handy at this moment.

"All right," resumed Dries. "Now, you'll find that the steering won't be too easy. When we get close, there'll be all kinds of currents, pulling us this way and that. Try to keep in the middle, both with your steering-oar and by telling me which oar to pull on. When we're almost in that gap, tell me to ship my oars and you slide down from the poop into the boat. That's important. The steering-oar will only hinder us when we go through, so be sure to get it out of the water and to get your own weight down into the boat."

"Wouldn't it be better if I took the oars and you did the steering?" I asked, frightened by the responsibility he was giving me.

Dries looked up at me, a mixture of reproach and understanding in his blue eyes. "Zippie," he said softly, "I'm not giving you the hardest part! Sure, the steering is difficult, but once we get through this gap, it needs a good oarsman to stay with the current and row with it instead of at odd angles to it. We won't have time to change places. Won't you trust me?"

"Of course I trust you," I said gruffly, thoroughly ashamed, and we all took our places. We cast off.

By now quite a number of Russian soldiers were standing on the pontoon bridge, watching us with interest. Even more of them were congregating on the quay near the collapsed railway bridge, with several of them climbing over the welter of spans and girders to get a better view. "Just look at those monkeys," sneered Nell. "Do they want to see us drown or what?"

Dries, warmhearted from his recent friendship with the Russian officer, said, "Don't be silly, Baron. They know we're going to take a risk and they're probably betting about our chances. Let's give them a winner."

Nell wasn't convinced, but now, as we neared the gap in the bridge, there was no time for idle chatter. Sitting on the poop and holding on to the heavy steering-oar, I felt contrary currents buffetting us around and kept shouting to Dries, "Pull hard on starboard now! Harder! Port now, more, more! Starboard again, easy now—little bit portside. Okay, we're in it now. Just keep her even!" I hardly had to tell him we were in it. All of us could feel the jolt of the boat as she picked up speed the second she got caught in the main stream that was pouring through the gap. Dries was sitting there with the oars full out, steadying the boat, his anxious eyes never leaving my face. In a flash I realised that indeed he had given me the easier job; I, at least, could see where we were going, but he had his back towards the danger and could only rely on my commands! I waited till I could distinguish the rivet heads on the first twisted girder, then yelled, "Pull your oars in!" I lifted my steering-oar clear out of the water and, holding on to it with all my strength, slid down from the poop and half-way into the boat.

A great cheer went up from the Russians on the quay and the bridge, the "Monty" was pitching wildly, and Dries had his oars out again, trying to steady us and steer us to quieter waters. Obviously we were not *kaput.* I turned round and joined Nell and Joke in some cheerful waving at the Russians. We had to hand it to them, for they didn't begrudge us our small triumph; they waved and hollered at us till we disappeared from view on the now fast-running current.

After a while we had lunch and I took over the oars again, for Dries was still feeling ill. Joke and Nell were in the grip of the reaction to our trek on foot, which would have been an easy hike for any well-fed person in good training, but had been a severe strain on our starved bodies and weakened muscles. I was feeling fit enough, however, and thoroughly enjoyed this slow voyage, the rhythmic creaking of the row-locks, the gentle breathing of the wide river, the majestic sweep of the wide land around me, the varied bird-life whenever the river wound its way through woods. Quite often I would see falcons, buzzards, and ospreys circling and planing overhead and, looking up at them and watching their movements, I would feel just as free and full of vitality as they were.

As we emerged from one of these woods, I glanced round and saw a sight that made me bring the boat swiftly to the bank and tell my friends to sit up and watch the fun. Just ahead of us, three Russian soldiers had come to the bank with a herd of about twenty horses. One soldier, naked astride his mount, was already in the water with three more horses swimming around him, and we saw the other two throw off their clothes and jump bareback on the nearest horse and drive the herd into the water. And now the river was alive with their laughter and their joyous shouts, the thrashing of the horses, the graceful movement of great glistening black and brown bodies among which the three naked men looked small as children. Quietly we sat and watched.

"God, this is splendid," said Joke softly, "I wish I were a painter!"

"You'd have to be a damn' good painter to catch the beauty and the movement," mused Nell.

We waited till they had finished their swim and the horses, stamping and pawing, whinnying and snorting, had climbed back on the bank. Then we pushed ourselves into the current again. As we came slowly by, we saw the soldiers dress quickly and mount again; then the whole herd went galloping off through the meadows.

"You know," said Dries thoughtfully, "I'm beginning to like these Russkis more and more."

"So do I," I laughed, "But not from too close by!"

Shortly afterwards it began to drizzle, and when we spotted a Dutch barge, at four-thirty, we were all ready to consider our day's work done even though there were several hours of daylight left. The prospect of another Dutch reception was too tempting, while the prospect of getting soaked in the rain for the sake of a few more miles held no attraction at all. So we rowed over and as soon as we had shouted, "Hollanders," an elderly couple appeared on deck and threw us a line. Ten minutes later we were sitting in another cosy kitchen, our cold hands cupped around mugs of hot cocoa.

Our hosts were a tall, grizzled skipper named Dirk Broekhuizen and his small, lively wife. They owned their barge and together did all the work on it, although both must have been around sixty. During the first four years of the War, they had managed, through various dodges, pretences, and illegal moves, to escape the German draft and work only on the Dutch rivers. But in September 1944 the Nazis had caught up with them, and there had been a choice of going to prison and losing their barge, or taking the barge to Germany and working for the Nazis. Regretfully, they chose the latter. They had been through several bombardments and seen plenty of fighting in towns farther downstream. Towards the very end of the War the tugboat that was towing them upstream had been sunk by a direct artillery hit, and since the Broekhuizens, unlike Asmus and Hartmans, had no auxiliary motor, they were stuck where they were—not at all in a convenient place, for it was an hour's walk to the village of Dommitzsch, the only place to buy such supplies as bread, milk, and meat. Mother Broekhuizen made this trip three times a week, for the skipper himself was slightly deaf and, as she said with a fond laugh, "He can't handle those Huns like I can!" It was bad enough, she continued, to have to spend all their hard-earned German money for a few necessities and to be sent from pillar to post for food coupons that were changed every few days. Her husband would never realise how everybody was out to cheat him, and anyway it was better to have a man in charge of the barge at all times.

They were a delightful couple, with the cunning, the shrewdness, the single-minded will to survival, but also the open hospitality, the piety, and the earthy sense of humour that mark the peasant stock of Europe, no matter what their nationality. They prayed humbly and seriously before the dinner of pancakes with bacon and raisins that they offered us, then teased the pants off Dries for travelling around with three girls. They waxed quite righteous in telling us that the Red Army was no better than the Hitler Army—"They're both uncivilised peoples, you know"—and then gleefully explained the various uncivilised tricks they had employed to hide and safeguard their obviously plentiful stores when their barge was looted, first by fleeing Germans, then by Russian troops.

"I've got enough flour here to make bread for months," confided the little woman, "but if I can get bread from the Huns, I'd rather take it from them. Their dirty money won't be worth anything a year from now, you mark my words!"

After dinner, while my three friends were nodding with fatigue over their cups of tea, I helped Mother Broekhuizen carry up an assortment of pillows, comforters, and blankets from their sleeping quarters to the little parlour; while the skipper pushed all the furniture into a corner she and I spread a big comfortable bed-for-four on the floor.

"It's a shame," she chuckled, "three young girls like you— you should have five young men with you; that way you'd have some choice!"

Back in the kitchen the skipper had the good idea of giving

K

us each a couple of aspirins with another cup of hot tea. Then
he folded his brown, muscle-knotted hands again and said an
evening prayer, and although none of us was particularly
religious, we were all moved by the earnest and personal way
in which he spoke to God.

"If there is a God," said Dries, while he was winding up the
alarm clock after we had all comfortably established ourselves
on the parlour floor, "I hope sincerely He takes care of people
like these."

We agreed.

The alarm went off at 6 a.m., but rain was pouring down and
we snuggled back under the blankets. Half an hour later Nell,
who was next to a porthole, said, "Okay, all of you, the sky is
getting lighter. We'd better get up." Our hosts had apparently
tiptoed through our quarters while we were still sound asleep;
they had hot coffee ready for us when we climbed up, still
sleepy-eyed, to the kitchen. They laughed at the way we
ploughed into the breakfast of Dutch rye bread with cheese
and honey; then they helped us stow our luggage into the
"Monty". Leaving the skipper behind, Mother Broekhuizen
decided to take advantage of our boat as far as Dommitzsch
and came aboard with her shopping-bag. It was eight-fifteen
when we cast off and nine o'clock when we arrived at Dommitzsch.

We decided that we might as well go ashore with Mother
Broekhuizen and see whether our food coupons and money
were worth anything. Accordingly, Nell and I left the boat
with Joke and Dries and ventured into the village. But, as we
had suspected, our food coupons weren't worth the paper they
were printed on, and our money, although genuine enough,
wouldn't buy anything without coupons. Finally we lined up
at the town hall and, after half an hour's wait, were given a
coupon for three and a half pounds of bread. No meat, no eggs,
no milk. So we said good-bye and thanks to the skipper's wife
and hurried back to the river.

Dries, feeling fine again, took over the oars. The rest of us wrapped ourselves in blankets and tarpaulins, for, although the rain had stopped, the sky was low and threatening and the wind blew watery and cold. I was sitting on the poop, giving an occasional steering direction to Dries and busying myself by cutting tobacco-leaves into small slivers, which I stored in an empty cocoa-tin the Broekhuizens had given us. Because of the wind, I could only handle very small quantities at a time, but I was in no hurry; slowly I got the tin filled and a supply of cigarettes rolled. The banks of the Elbe became wilder, with more and denser woods, stretches of swampland, and wide expanses of grassland innocent of any farms or signs of human life.

"I don't know what these Nazis wanted all that *Lebensraum* for," remarked Nell. "There's room for a million of them here."

It was a quiet, uneventful day. We went a distance of twenty miles before we saw the first Russian soldiers of the day. They guarded a high and narrow steel bridge that miraculously had escaped destruction, but they made no difficulties for us. After the usual pantomime of eager interest and sad disappointment over our demijohn, we continued on our way and Dries and I changed places. Towards six in the evening we were on the outskirts of the town of Wittenberg. There were no barges in sight and we decided to try our luck here instead of going to the town proper, where we might run into the trouble of having to register, or—worse—being herded into a camp. There was a small dent in the bank, where the water was shallow and half-hidden under the overhanging branches of two big weeping willows. We steered the boat into this natural hiding-place and Nell and Dries disembarked to scout around for shelter, while Joke and I packed our belongings and loaded them onto the Tank and Pram.

After half an hour, our two friends were back. "There's been a lot of fighting in this town," reported Nell. "There are more ruins than houses, and there isn't a single whole window left. But we've found a place anyway, at the house of a widow named Richter."

"She's another Mrs Nut," added Dries, "but she has a fairly big house with a roof on it, and that's more than most of them can say around here."

We lifted the Tank and the Pram onto dry land. Dries dragged the *Montgomery* as close to the trunk of one of the willows as he could and secured it with the chain and padlock. For extra measure, he threw a few loose branches over the boat to hide it, and we set off along a narrow road that led to the first shells of houses near the water. Nell hadn't exaggerated. Most of the buildings were crumbled piles of bricks and beams; of the few that were still standing, the walls were pockmarked with bullet-holes, the windows gaping or boarded up with planks and cardboard. Dries led us through a winding street, where the cracked and broken pavement threatened to over-turn the Tank several times, and stopped at a house that indeed looked better than the others, although one corner of it was completely gone and not a single window had any glass panes left.

The widow Richter was even crazier than Mrs Nut, yet smart enough to put us to work immediately, dragging furni-ture from the damaged part of the house to the rooms that had remained intact, blocking broken windows with cupboards and up-ended trunks and nailing heavy draperies over others. For nearly two hours we pushed and carried and shoved and slaved while she kept up a constant patter of talk, partly incompre-hensible but extremely precise in the directions of what she wanted done. It turned out that very few people were still living in this part of town, which had been officially evacuated, but that she was determined to hang on in order to save her possessions.

Finally, satisfied with our work, she showed us to a bedroom, where earlier we had blocked the window with a tall wardrobe. It had two fully-made beds. After she had left us, we partly unblocked the window again, preferring a little light and fresh air to the supposed safety, and too tired to go out and build a fire among the ruins, had a cold supper of bread and tinned meat, then gratefully climbed between the clean sheets. Even

Joke had now become used enough to civilisation to be grateful for a soft bed!

Anxious about "Monty", Dries had set the alarm for 5 a.m. When it rang, he shot out of bed and into his clothes, telling us he was going to go ahead to see that the boat was safe and that we should follow him as soon as we had packed the wagons. About half an hour later we pushed the wardrobe back in front of the window, carried out the Tank and the Pram, shouted good-bye to our hostess, and went down to the river; there, to our relief, we found Dries waiting in the boat, which he had neatly scrubbed out. It was raining and we retreated to the first ruin, where we could keep an eye on the boat; huddled together under a remnant of roof, we made a fire among the rubble of bricks and used our last coffee to make a hot, strong brew for our breakfast. After we had eaten we sat and smoked till a little after seven, when the rain stopped and we could cast off once more.

It was cold again. When we came to the Wittenberg bridge, the expected bullet whistled through the air, but, not seeing the sentry, we pulled up to the wrong side, and a second and third bullet followed until we finally spotted him crawling out of a covered foxhole on the other bank. He was a pleasant fellow, though, who spoke enough German to tell us that he, personally, had no objection to letting us through but that he didn't think we would go far, for the American lines started at Dessau. He went carefully through our luggage to make sure that we had no weapons, but did not take anything from us.

A little farther on, another destroyed railway bridge was lying in the water, but it did not dam up the river as badly as the one in Torgau, and we manœuvred through it quite easily. Dries looked at his map and estimated that it was about thirty miles to Dessau. With a little luck we could reach the Americans that same day! Full of optimism, Dries and I took half-hour turns at the oars and rowed all the way, so that in spite of the strong head wind we were making good progress. Towards noon, we had done twelve miles and were nearing the

town of Coswig. We had been quite close to it an hour earlier,
but at that point the Elbe made a three-and-a-half-mile loop
through a dense, tall forest that grew right up to the river
banks. After Wittenberg we had seen only one party of
Russians, and they were too busy fishing with dynamite, setting
off the charges under water and then scooping up the dead fish
that came to the surface, to pay any attention to us.

I was at the oars when we came out of the forest. Noticing
to our right a kind of ferrying-place with a wooden shack and
a number of small boats tied up, I surmised that this probably
marked the town of Coswig; but I was also watching the
majestic circling of three ospreys over the stretch of river we
had just passed through, and I didn't pay much attention to
the ferry post. My three friends were all curled up under blankets because of the cold. When I drew even with the ferry, a
bullet came singing past. It was so wide of its mark, however,
that I wasn't sure it was meant for us. Anyway, there was no
bridge, so why should I stop? We weren't much of a target;
maybe I could just ignore the shooting. Pulling a little harder
on the oars, I slid by. This time a whole burst of bullets sizzled
into the water; Nell and Dries sat up and asked, "What's going
on, Zip?"

"I don't know," I answered, "seems they want us to stop, but
it's only a ferry post, not a bridge. Their shooting is pretty wild
though, maybe we can get through."

"Don't try it," said Nell sharply, looking at the wooden shack,
"there's a whole lot of them, and they're yelling and waving
at us."

A new hail of bullets, closer this time. "Pull in, Zip," said
Dries in his captain's voice. "You're being foolish. Look, they're
sending a guy with a tommy gun after us!"

I could see as well as he that a Russian soldier on a bicycle
was frantically pedalling along a path that followed the river
bank, holding his tommy gun over the handlebars. It so happened that a breakwater stuck out into the river at this point
and, unable to row against the current, I had to make my way

round it to pull up to the bank. But our comrade on the bike suspected foul play and managed a burst over the handlebars without interrupting his speed. Thanks probably to a rut in the path the shots fell short, although two or three bullets nicked the side of the boat.

Damn it, I thought bitterly to myself, there had to be a path along the bank at this point, and a breakwater too. Without those, we might have got away.

Reluctantly I brought the "Monty" to the bank, and a minute later the panting Russian was telling us to go back to the ferry post right away! He probably didn't realise that none of us was strong enough to row against the stream, but after some excited talking and gesticulating back and forth, he allowed Dries and me to walk to the ferry post, while he kept a menacing tommy gun trained on Nell and Joke, who were guarding the boat.

This time, however, our slip of paper with the magic words had lost its power. Dries and I did our best at the post and had no trouble explaining our purpose, for one of the six Russians there spoke fluent German and was very correct and understanding. Nevertheless, he stuck to his "*nyet*". We had to bring the boat back to the ferry for inspection, and if we wanted to continue, well, the only thing we could do was ask the Kommandant in Coswig for a special permit. There was nothing to do but obey. This was no private party of Russkis bent on their own pleasures; they were official sentries doing their duty. Moreover, I had now taken a good look at the small boats tied up here and had an awful suspicion that they were the boats of people who had preceded us down the Elbe.

We returned to the *Montgomery* to explain the situation to Joke and Nell. After discussing it, Nell and I set off for the Kommandant's office, leaving the heavy work of pulling the boat round the breakwater and up to the post to Joke and Dries. Tramping the mile towards the centre of the town, Nell and I figured that this would probably cost us three to four hours, and that we might be forced to spend the night somewhere near here and not reach Dessau till the next day. Alas, we were still being too optimistic. At the town hall we were told that the Kommandant would not be there till 4 p.m.

With two hours to while away, we decided to see if we could get any bread, for our own supply was down to half a loaf. From the town hall we were sent to another office, then to another one, without any success. Next we met a group of Frenchmen who tried to put us wise. They told us that there was no way to get any food in Coswig except by going to the camps. They were in an exclusively French camp, they said, but there was another one a mile farther on where Hollanders and all others were interned. Both camps were run by the Russians. They obligingly showed us the way and we trudged a mile along the dusty road to the French camp, where another polite Frenchman explained that we could not get any food there, and then another mile to the so-called "General Camp".

This proved to be a collection of long wooden barracks plus an assortment of odd hutments, tents, and foxholes, inhabited by a motley multitude of ex-slave labourers and workers who had voluntarily come to Germany. Our first reaction was to turn away immediately; only the fact that we needed both information and food made us persist till we had found the "office", where a blowsy Russian girl and an arrogant Dutch boy (whom we distrusted because he wore parts of a Nazi uniform) told us that the only way to get food was to register in the camp, which we would have to do anyway because there was no other place to go.

Disgusted, Nell and I turned away and went back to the town hall. But the news there was just as bad. The Kommandant would not be back today after all, and would probably be too busy to see us tomorrow. Outside again, I happened to see the German-speaking Russian whom Dries and I had met at the ferry, walking towards us from the direction of the river. Now that he was alone, he spoke more freely. We were trying the impossible, he advised us; not a single boat had gone through this post since he had been stationed here three weeks ago. Whether we saw the Kommandant or not, we would have to go to the camp and wait till there was an organised exchange. "What do you mean, exchange?" we asked, and he answered, "Well, every ten days or so, we send over a group of you people and then the Americans send back a group of Russians they're holding over there."

"Are you sure of that?" we asked him. "Are you sure we won't have to go to Odessa if we go to this camp?"

He bridled a little at that. "What's wrong with going to Odessa?" he asked.

"Nothing," we said quite honestly, "except that it would take so long and we're in a hurry to get home. You see, we don't even know if our families are alive, or our homes still there, or anything." Thereupon he relented and assured us that, from this town at least, repatriation would be direct and not by way of Odessa. "Then why can't you give us a pass for our boat?" we insisted. "It's only twenty miles or so and you wouldn't have to keep us in a camp."

But he just shrugged and said, "We have orders. You'd better go to the camp."

Defeated, Nell and I walked back to the river and told our friends that we had to abandon the "Monty" and go to the camp. Dries and Joke, who had finally managed to get the boat back to the post and were sitting there waiting for us, did not argue. We trusted each other implicitly, and they knew that we had done our utmost to get round this obstacle. Sadly and silently we went through the familiar motions of unloading our gear from the "Monty" and packing it onto the little wagons. We said a last farewell to our *Montgomery*, which had served us so proudly, if only for four short days, and left her in the indifferent care of the Russian sentries at the ferry post. Then, thoroughly dejected, we started to pull the Pram and the Tank along the three miles to the place we had so much tried to avoid: a Russian "displaced persons" camp.

Chapter Seven

WEARILY we trudged the last mile uphill, but before we arrived we sat down at the side of the road, and to give ourselves courage ate our last bread with a thick covering of tinned meat. A 6 p.m. we were at the dirty little office where the same nonchalant Russian girl wrote some Russian characters in a dog-eared ledger. Apparently they represented the sound of our names to her; she didn't ask us to spell them and we didn't volunteer, for the old mistrust about registering one's name was still with us. Then she informed us that there was no more room in the barracks and we would have to sleep somewhere outside. When we asked about food, she answered that we could return for the regular distribution three days later. Our spirits still lower, we wandered disconsolately into the camp, looking for a place to spend the night.

The camp itself consisted of nine wooden barracks lined up in rows of three, with rectangular fields of grass in between. At right angles to the barracks stood two wooden shacks that housed the office, the mess hall, and the kitchens. But around this Spartan and fairly neat layout was an enormous, colourful ring of the oddest variety of encampments we had ever set eyes on. There were sod huts and huts made out of woven branches; shacks of galvanised iron and of flimsy boards; pup tents and covered foxholes. There were people living underneath farm wagons, with blankets draped between the wheels for walls; there were people crawling under, in, and on top of small

trucks. Spaced fairly regularly throughout this belt of varie-
gated gypsy life stood little potbellied stoves, each with a few
people around it, cooking or waiting their turn. There had been
a wooden fence surrounding it all, but only bits and pieces of
it were now left, most of it doubtless having disapeared into
the stoves. And, oddly, here and there among this mass of
humanity stood a quiet horse or a mule, tethered to a pole, the
wheel of a truck, or whatever happened to be handy.

Forlornly we picked our way through it all. There didn't
seem to be even a few free yards of ground anywhere, much
less any available shelter. The rectangular grass fields between
the barracks were so conspicuously empty that we didn't have
to be told that camping there was forbidden. In spite of the
keen disappointment of that day, I found something oddly
appealing in the incredible scene around us. "I always wanted
to be a gypsy as a kid," I said to Nell, who was pulling the
Pram with me. "It looks as if I've finally got my chance."

Finally, behind the last barracks of the middle row, we came
across two friendly Dutch boys, who showed us the small truck
they were using for sleeping quarters. The two of them slept in
the back, they told us, and two Belgians were using the cab,
but if we wanted the space under the truck, we were welcome.
Maybe we could attach a blanket to the side and stretch it
over two poles; that would give us some extra space. They
were right. At least we'd be dry if it rained.

"Have you eaten anything?" asked the Dutch boys.

We answered that we had been told we could not get food
for three days.

"That's true," one of them said, "but I'll tell you what. At the
far end of the kitchen building there's the entrance to the
potato cellar. It's usually open. You just slip in there when no
Russians are looking and you can take all you want."

"Thanks, pal," I said. Picking up my big kerchief, I set off
towards the kitchen to organise our evening meal. It proved
very simple. There was nobody around when I went in, and I
waited quietly in the semi-darkness, my kerchief heavy with

potatoes, till the boots of a Russian soldier which were visible when I peeked out had sauntered away. I made a tour among several of the potbellied stoves and under each of them placed four potatoes in the hot ashes that spilled from their bottoms, covering them carefully and noting the location of the stoves in my mind. When I rejoined my friends, they had unpacked the tarpaulin and were trying to attach it to the truck's side with rusty nails from the picket fence. I helped for a while, then returned to my potatoes. I found them nicely done; rather to my surprise, not a single one of the sixteen was missing.

When we had eaten, a tall, blond, blue-eyed young man who had been watching us from a little distance came over and said, "You're Dutch too, aren't you?" We nodded and invited him to sit down. Over a cigarette we exchanged news. His name was Jos. Like so many young Dutchmen, he had been caught in one of the Nazi raids for slave labour and brought to Germany in January 1945. When he heard that we had come down the Elbe, he said, "Then you don't have to stay under this truck. There's a whole room full of skippers who came down the Elbe; it's a kind of club. They'll help you out. I'll go and talk to them." With that he got up and walked away. We brightened up considerably. Among those skippers must be the barge-hands from the *Codam 85* and the others that Asmus and Hartmans had been talking about. In a world like ours, this meant old friends, even if we had never met them.

Jos returned shortly and said, "It's okay, they'll fix you up. Pack up your stuff and come along, I'll show you." As we quickly ripped the tarpaulin off the truck and stowed our gear helter-skelter into the wagons, he added apologetically, "I'd invite you into the room I'm in, but they're a pretty lousy bunch. I only stay there because a bunk inside is better than these rat-holes outside."

Dries, who had been searching his memory, now looked up at Jos and asked, "Look, were you in the Merchant Marine by any chance?"

Jos's face broke into a smile as wide and sunny as an ocean beach on a brilliant June morning. "You bet, mate!" he said. "I thought there was something familiar about either your face or your name, but I couldn't figure out which."

The two men shook hands solemnly, and immediately fell into excited conversation, trying to pin down whether they actually had worked on the same ship some six years ago or whether they had merely heard about each other from mutual friends. From that moment on, Jos became the full-fledged fifth member of our gang.

The "skippers' room" proved to be in the first barracks in the middle row; before we went in I noticed with satisfaction that it was a pretty handy location in relation to the potato cellar. When the blanket that covered the open doorway was lifted by Jos, a raucous cheer went up, and we saw twelve more or less hirsute faces eagerly sizing us up, some craned from the top of double-decker bunks, others looking up from the floor. Sitting on the big table in the middle of the room were an extremely portly, greying man in his fifties and a slight blond youth who looked hardly older than seventeen.

"Everybody at attention!" shouted a voice from an upper bunk. "Here's women that aren't hussies!"

"Welcome, welcome," boomed the portly gentleman from the table, "we hear you came down the Elbe!"

Nell was our spokesman. She was the only one among us who had any experience at public speaking, and although our public here was small, to us it was an extremely important one. At that moment we wanted nothing so much as to be accepted in the "Elbe Club". Nell did a splendid job. In a few succinct phrases she summed up our resistance and prison careers, then gave a short account of our trek from Waldheim to Coswig. There was applause when she came to our river journey, but it was quickly shushed when Nell managed to get in a few feeling words about how Hollanders had to stick together wherever they were, that we had found that spirit along the river and were delighted to find it again in this rag-tag camp.

The applause after that was very convincing, but the skippers had got the point. One of them, a short pug-nosed man who introduced himself as Dorus, quickly explained, "Look, kids, this is the way it is. Every one of these barracks has ten rooms plus a washroom and a latrine. Each room is supposed to have twelve bunks, except that most of them don't, for the Italian labourers that lived here in the first place smashed a lot of bunks for firewood. Those poor macaroni eaters, you know, they weren't used to cold climates. As you can see, we have eleven bunks here. Some rooms have ten, some only eight. Now the Russkis have made three rules for this camp, and they aren't bad rules at that. One is that all the stoves have to be outside—you probably saw them. Second, no people can camp on these grass fields between the barracks. That sounds silly, but it isn't, really. We use those fields for a lot of things: soccer games and boxing matches—you'll soon see for yourself. It's nice to have a little open space available. The last rule is that no room can hold more people than there are bunks. Now that's a lot of baloney, so don't worry your heads about it. We've been twelve in here for the last week and we can easily make it fourteen. It's impossible for them to check, and they're not breaking their necks over it anyhow. Pops here"—with a gesture towards the portly gentleman who was still sitting on the table—"has been sleeping on the table all the time. He prefers it that way. Now Tony is going to join him and Johan says he'd kind of prefer to sleep on the floor. So how about two of you girls taking those empty bunks?"

Dorus had maintained a businesslike tone until the last sentence, when the hopeful entreaty in his voice gave him away. It was obvious that the presence of two young women in his quarters would make his camp life a lot less dreary. Joke gave him the right answer: "Of course we'd like to," she exclaimed and forthwith threw herself on the bunk in the corner that Tony had vacated.

Dries was whispering to Nell, "You'd better take that upper bunk and keep an eye on Joke. These are nice fellows but you can never tell——" when we heard Jos's voice behind us asking quietly, "What about the other two? You said you could take care of all of them?"

"Sure we can, sure," answered Dorus, reluctantly taking his eyes off Joke. "We've arranged that with the Northerners down the corridor." He hustled over to us and looked Dries and me over from top to toe. "Sorry I can't keep you here also," he said softly. "You can see that it would be rather crowded. But you can leave all your stuff here and consider this room your day quarters. There's always at least one of us around and your gear will be safe. And of course you'll come and eat with us too. But there's a room full of Northerners in the next barrack and we have a bargain with them—they'll give you sleeping-space. Come on, I'll take you there."

"What do you mean, Northerners?" I asked, as we followed him down the barrack's corridor.

"Oh, you know," he answered airily, "they're all farm-hands from Groningen, but they're damn' good guys."

Though Holland is a tiny country there is a wide variety of dialect. I knew by Dorus's accent that he came from Limburg, our most southern province, while the people he was taking us to came from the northernmost one of Groningen. Religious difference helps to keep alive this difference in accent: north of the big rivers the Dutch are generally Protestant; to the south the majority are Roman Catholic.

Dorus led us into the next barracks and lifted another blanket door. At first sight, this room seemed even more crowded than the skippers' room, but I saw that this was because here they had benches at their long table. When we came in, most of the occupants were seated on these benches, presenting us with a solid row of six angular backs topped by blond heads, while five angular blue-eyed faces stared at us from the opposite side. "Here's your new customers," said Dorus, by way of introduction. "Just show them where they can sleep and they'll come back later."

One of the powerful frames on the bench in front of me

stirred, got up, vaulted the bench, and came over with outstretched hand. "Glad to have you," he said slowly. "Hope you
won't mind sleeping on straw." This room did have its full
complement of twelve bunks, all of them occupied, but in addition there was a nice thick spread of straw in one corner. Our
host showed us this and said, "There's only two fellows sleeping there now and we think there's room enough for four.
What do you think?"

Dries looked it over judiciously and answered, "We've slept in
smaller places with more people," and, turning to the room in
general, said with feeling, "We're surely glad you're willing to
have us!"

My mother came from the Groningen province and I was
familiar enough with the dialect to put at least a touch of it
into my language when I added, "I'll be very proud to sleep
here. What better protection could I have than fourteen
Groningers?" This produced a guffaw that bellowed around
the room, and I decided we were accepted.

It was late that night when Dries and I, in pyjamas and
wrapped in our blankets, made our way from the skippers'
room to the Northerners'. We had a lot to talk over with the
skippers. Actually, only eight of them were skippers; but they
were the very ones Asmus and Hartmans had told us about,
and of course we had to compare notes about our common
experiences. How had they fared at the Torgau bridge? Had
they seen the Broekhuizens? And so on. Some tall tales were
spun that night, and the fall of the river at Torgau gradually
increased to about twelve feet.

We were offered a late supper of mashed potatoes and tinned
meat, which we gratefully accepted; with some difficulty we
discovered who the minority of four non-skippers in the room
were. There was Johan the gym coach, a carpenter named
Pete, a construction worker also named Pete, and an odd-jobs
man named Henk. They had earned their badge in the
skippers' room by coming down from Wittenberg in two stolen
canoes. This satisfied me; I had seen two-rowing-boats and two

canoes at the ferry post. That accounted for all the people in this room and left only one boat unexplained. "Tell me," I asked, "there was a white-painted rowing-boat at the ferry post. Light one, but it had a rudder and oars. Who brought that down?"

They all laughed at my ignorance. "That's the Russians' patrol boat," they answered. "Usually they have it on the river all day long, manned by three chaps, one at the rudder, one at the oars, one at the tommy gun. That's how we were stopped. Weren't they out there when you came through?" Thereupon we had to tell the story of how we were actually stopped, which drew a lot of conflicting comment. "You should have gone right through!" "You did well in stopping, you might have been shot to pieces!" "You might have made it around the bend!" "What are you fellows complaining about, we've got ourselves some girls, haven't we?"

We gathered that we had happened to come along at a time when the Russians, tired of patrolling an empty river, had decided to have a little lunch ashore and that we had taken them unawares. With a little more rowing prowess on my part, we might have got through. We might also have been shot to pieces. Had I been right? Should I have pulled harder on my oars? I was still worrying about it when I snuggled into my place in the straw between Dries and a complete stranger.

The next day was May 26, 1945, my twenty-ninth birthday. Ever since our liberation my most fervent wish had been to spend this birthday at home—for the first time since 1941. Instead I found myself waking up with straw in my hair, in a room with fifteen men, some still snoring loudly, others sitting half-dressed on their bunks, a few stirring around the big table in preparation for breakfast. Dries and I got up, folded our blankets and, in our pyjamas, walked over to the washroom with our toothbrushes and soap. It was only about eight o'clock, but already the washroom was bedlam. There was a trough running round most of the room, with cold-water taps spaced

L

about six feet apart. That meant about sixteen taps, and when we came in there were already about forty people milling around. In the middle of the room was a big cast-iron kettle to boil laundry in, but it had no tap of its own and apparently had to be filled from the wall taps.

Dries and I waited half an hour before we could find space at one faucet for a quick wash of face and hands, a brushing of teeth, and a pulling of wet combs through our tangled hair. Thus partly spruced up, we walked over to the skippers' room. And there my thoroughly vile mood changed instantly. Dries had hardly lifted the curtain when various tenors, baritones, and bassos broke into the Dutch equivalent of "Happy Birthday to You," accompanied by Dorus on a harmonica. Joke and Nell were sitting on their bunks, not adding their sopranos to this uproarious chorus, but obviously eager to see how I would take it. And there was more. Johan had gone out into the fields and picked a bunch of daisies, poppies, and cornflowers, whose red, white, and blue stuck up proudly from a jagged tin can in the middle of the table. Pops had been prevailed upon to part with his last real coffee, and the good, strong morning-smell of it struggled valiantly with the sleeping-smell of a packed roomful of people.

It touched me deeply. It was nothing like the homecoming I had dreamed of, but in its own way it was almost better. I had wanted to celebrate the bond with my own family; instead I celebrated the bond with my own nation, represented by an odd combination of people from all corners of Holland and from all walks of life. Joke ran off to find Jos, and eventually we all sat down to a breakfast of real coffee, a big dish of groats cooked in salted water, plus the scrapings from meat cans, and —my birthday present from the skippers—a whole loaf of bread.

After this emotional start to the day, we had to become practical again. I returned to the potato cellar and emerged once more with a kerchief-full, which we hid away in the skippers' room. Then we started looking for sanitary facilities. As Dries and I had already found out that morning, they were very inadequate. The barracks had originally been built for about one thousand Italian labourers at the time when Germany and Italy were Axis partners and Germany could get Italian labour for practically nothing. Now there were about four thousand displaced persons using the same facilities. They had not been built to include women in the first place, and the Russian conquerors had done nothing to improve things. Each barrack had its row of eight doorless cubicles with toilet bowls and eight urinals on the opposite wall. The washrooms had no doors, either.

"Let's take to the fields," said Nell, and that first morning we did. But the fields, already being used by all the outdoor dwellers around us, gave hardly any privacy, and weren't handy enough for the sudden upheavals our insides still suffered. We returned to the camp and, on closer inspection, found that one of the barracks latrines had been closed off by the Russians. Locating this from the outside wasn't difficult, and Dries did some expert jemmying to open the window. We all climbed in and inspected the premises. Four of the eight toilet bowls had clogged and the drains had packed up, but the other four were in perfect working shape and would give us the privacy we wanted. Surreptitiously we crept out of the window one by one, then closed it to about an eighth of an inch from the sash; from the outside it still looked closed. Now all we had to do was keep our secret to ourselves and make sure that our comings and goings through the window would remain unnoticed.

The question of where to wash was harder. All the washrooms were alike and without doors, and there was no water available elsewhere. "We could walk down to the Elbe and swim when it gets a little warmer," suggested Dries. "You know, at that place where the big loop through the forest starts. That can't be more than three miles from here."

"We could," said Joke, "but what about cold and rainy days? I'd like to keep as clean as possible. This place has almost as much vermin as the prison."

In prison, with assiduous care and daily inspection of our clothes, we had managed to keep ourselves free of lice, though we fought a losing battle against the armies of fleas and bed-bugs that invaded our cells. Since then we had been happily free of them, but Joke was right: a camp like this was sure to be crawling with vermin.

"I guess the best thing is to use the washrooms at night when everybody is asleep," said Nell.

"Or have Dries and Jos stand guard at the door at some odd hour in the afternoon when they aren't much in use," I added.

When we returned to the skippers' room, we were told that we had to go to the Russian doctor for an examination, that everybody who wanted to go on an exchange transport had to have a slip of paper from the doctor. Accordingly we set off for the big villa down the road, where the Russians connected with our camp had their quarters. Here Dries was shoved into one room and we three girls into another, which proved to hold already about twenty women, some seated on benches along the wall, others standing in line. An imperious Russian girl made us join the line and told us to undress from the waist down. Looking past the line, I could see a doctor in a dirty white coat standing at a long table covered with a dirty sheet, and suddenly realised that this so-called medical examination was nothing but inspection for venereal disease. I knew damn' well we had no venereal disease and that if there was ever a likely spot to pick up something, it was right there on that filthy sheet and from a doctor who handled one woman after another without washing his hands. Some of them were sent back to the benches, others were given a slip of paper and could leave. Furious as we were at this distasteful performance, if we wanted the slip of paper there was no choice but to go through with it, and one by one we climbed onto the table for the inspection, which lasted only seconds.

That afternoon, while we were lying in the sun on the grass field between the barracks, Jos, after much prodding, told us some more about himself. He had been a member of a resistance group that specialised in sabotage, and after September 1944, when southern Holland had been liberated, he had become a contact man between the Dutch resistance and the Allied armies, crossing the rivers back and forth on dark nights. It was pure luck that when he got caught in the streets of Rotterdam during one of the Nazis' periodic raids for slave labour, the Germans had been too disorganised to recognise his true identity, or he would have been shot on the spot.

He also told us more about the camp itself. His estimate was that about half its population consisted of ex-slave labourers, while the other half had come to Germany voluntarily, attracted by German promises of high wages and sometimes even by Nazi ideology. The latter half included all the women, of whom there were about three hundred. Jos was sure, too, that a small percentage of the men had enlisted in the German Army or the Storm Troopers; these, by being in the camp, hoped to return to their own countries without their treason being detected.

"But how are you going to pick them out?" asked Joke. He shrugged. "I guess that will be taken care of when they get to their own borders." He knew of no other political ex-prisoners in the camp, but then it was impossible to keep track of four thousand people. There were Belgians, Yugoslavs, Italians, Greeks, and Hollanders in the crowd; all one could do was accept anybody's story at face value—if, indeed, it was told in a language one could understand.

Nell took care of the cooking that evening; she proudly served us with pea soup and a birthday cake made from mashed potatoes and decorated with slivers of tinned meat. Dorus played some more on his harmonica. What with the continuous joking and kidding and the incredible stories told mostly by Pops and Dorus, it was, after all, a pleasant birthday evening.

As the days went by, we got to know the camp intimately. Although there were two or three sentries posted around it at all times, they let everybody wander freely in and out. They knew well enough that there was no other place for us to go and that nobody dared wander too far away for fear of missing the great chance of going home. The Russians in charge of the camp must have known also about the daily plundering expeditions that went on, but if it was not done too openly and the loot wasn't too big, they closed their eyes to it. The skippers took no part in these operations, for the simple reason that they didn't have to. Among them they had a large supply of tobacco-leaves, and, as tobacco was practically legal tender, they could exchange it for anything they wanted. In this way they had acquired a radio for their room; whenever we could get Radio Orange, the free Dutch radio which had broadcast from London during the War but was now located in Holland proper, we would listen breathlessly for news from home. Yet it chagrined us to hear the announcer describe the horrors of the Nazi concentration camps and prisons. It was all true enough, but couldn't he wait to tell these things till all living prisoners had returned? Didn't he realise that there were thousands of us wandering through Germany, unable to get home? Why make our families suffer through these stories of atrocities before they knew for sure whether we were alive or dead?

There were about two dozen Yugoslavs in the camp, who were always eating high off the hog, quite literally. They all wore Russian-type uniforms—probably they had fought with the Russians and been taken prisoner—and they would simply go to a German farm, present themselves as Russian soldiers, and commandeer whatever struck their fancy. One evening they came home with a whole slaughtered pig, and the next morning, in exchange for a small paper bag full of tobacco-leaves, I secured a big hunk of pork which lasted us for several days. After our third day in the camp, we had been given the wooden tags that entitled us to receive food from the camp kitchens. At noon we would get a quarter-pound chunk of dark, sour bread and a pint of soup, and the same again at six in the evening. The soup was very good, with plenty of meat and barley in it, but even so it wasn't enough to keep up with our tremendous appetites; after our own rice and dried peas had run out, we had to rely on either trading or stealing for our extras. I continued making daily trips to the potato-cellar and occasionally went farther afield to snatch a head of lettuce, a bunch of carrots, or a handful of tomatoes from those German vegetable gardens that I could approach undetected. We had all developed a craving for fresh greens, and we often had dreams in which we would run after crazily rolling oranges and apples that stayed for ever out of reach.

Most of our daylight hours in the camp were thus devoted to keeping ourselves properly fed: the hours of standing in line at the soup kitchens; the hours spent hunting for fuel for the outdoor stoves; the pleasant hours around those stoves, with some brew of our own bubbling merrily away while the potatoes cooked slowly in the ashes.

But there were other distractions. The weather continued warm and sunny; on most afternoons international soccer games were played on the fields between the barracks. Sometimes two or three would be under way at the same time: Italy–Belgium, Holland–Italy, and then Belgium–Holland. The spectators would drift from one game to the other, cheering their favourite team or their favourite players, and the players themselves drifted just as casually. Anybody who didn't like his opponents, the referee, or his team mates would wander over to the next field and join another team. There would frequently be thirteen on one side and ten on the other, but nobody minded. There was no time limit on the games, either. They would simply last till all the players were tired and left the field, or till some particularly choice insult started a friendly free-for-all in which the spectators joined.

On other afternoons, after we had carefully tracked down every rumour that this was "transport day" and found them all baseless, we would take the risk of leaving the camp for four hours and tramp through the fields to the bend in the Elbe where the forest started. There we would spend an hour or so swimming, washing ourselves from head to toe and drying in the hot sun. The atmosphere of freedom in this idyllic spot would lead Dries, Joke, and me to indulge in the wildest dreams of swimming across the river here one evening and then making our way on foot to Dessau. By sticking close to the forest we could always hide in it whenever there was danger, and although we would have to leave all our belongings behind, what did that matter? Once inside the American lines, surely we would have no more need for extra clothing and supplies?

But Nell would not hear of any such plans. It was crazy to risk our lives now, she maintained, and between here and Dessau we would be living targets for every sentry around.

Jos, who usually listened quietly to the whole discussion, would speak up and side with Nell. "It's too risky," he said. "The Russians have strict orders not to let anyone through, and I suspect that the Americans have their sentries out, too. Don't forget, there are quite a number of unsavoury characters, collaborators and so on, who would like to get out of here. Now that there are arrangements for an exchange, the Americans are bound to question anybody who tries it on his own. Maybe they shoot first, like our Russian comrades."

"Do you know of any exchange that has actually taken place?" we asked, and Jos answered, "Yes, a column of about five hundred Frenchies left the French camp the day before you arrived."

That gave us a little hope and patience again. Then one morning Nell woke up with her right leg swollen and mottled with bright red patches, and there were no more daring escapes planned. It gave her considerable pain whenever she tried to walk on it and although some salve supplied by Pops would ease the pain somewhat, she could do no more than hobble around from that day on. Whenever we went swimming in the Elbe, Nell had to stay behind. That took some of the pleasure out of it for us, and we took to washing late at night, when the washrooms, which had no electric light, were dark and deserted. One night we were in our usual corner and had just stripped and started to soap ourselves when a stranger with a candle appeared in the doorway. There was nothing we could do about him, so we just ignored him; after about five minutes of quiet contemplation he left, apparently satisfied. Another time Joke happened to notice a completely empty washroom during the afternoon. This was quite rare, for usually they were occupied all day long by clusters of people doing their laundry. Joke quickly rounded us all up and, while Dries and Jos stood guard in the doorway, we prepared ourselves for a good scrub. But we had figured without Dorus. He had seen us getting our towels and, at a critical moment, appeared between Jos and Dries with the cheerful proposition: "Hey, honeys, shall I scrub your backs?" Our two guards were so helpless with laughter that Dorus actually managed to get by them and take some vigorous swipes at us with a washcloth, before we could get serious enough to shoo him out again.

But nobody could stay angry with Dorus. He was so lovable and full of fun that he was known throughout the camp. Short and bow-legged, with his wrinkled, pug-nosed face and the curved pipe from which he was inseparable, he looked like one of Walt Disney's dwarfs. But he was a born leader and if anybody was homesick or downcast about the long delay in the camp, a little of Dorus's special brand of humour was all the medicine needed to cheer him up again. When he appeared on the soccer field to play, his pipe still firmly clenched between his teeth, a cheer would go up from players and spectators alike.

Whenever we were gathered together in the skippers' room, sitting on the bunks or crowded around the table, Dorus would start telling stories. All of his stories were off-colour but some were more so than others. When they got too outrageous, we would get up and say, "Dorus, we will have to leave if you go on like that," and immediately he would protest, "No, no, stay around. From now on I'll tell only stories for under the Christmas tree!" The next two or three would be quite tame by his standards, but then he would be off again. "Dorus, what did you do with the Christmas tree?" Joke asked once, and he

turned to her with genuine regret and amazement in his voice
and said, "I'm so sorry, baby, I must have pushed it aside."

We had quickly become friends with all the skippers and
non-skippers in the room, and had exchanged addresses so that
whoever got home first could pass the good word along. Most
of them had shown us pictures of their wives, sweethearts, and
children, but we had been in the camp at least five days and
were already quite familiar with Dorus's breathtaking love life
up and down the rivers of Europe, when he produced a wallet
and extricated some much-fingered snapshots of his wife and
teen-age daughter.

"You mean to say that you are married, Dorus?" asked Joke
incredulously.

"Of course, honey," he answered lightly. "When I get tired
of it all, I've got to have a place I can go home to and rest up,
don't I?" And that, according to Dorus, was that.

Yet Dorus, and the whole room full of skippers, were fiercely
protective of us. Every morning the Russian women who
worked in the kitchens would run through the barracks round-
ing up work details among the women in the camp, to
scrub the corridors and the washrooms and to clean up in the
kitchens. They tried at various times to get us out of the skippers's room, but each time they ran into a solid barrier of men,
who would shout at them, "Go get the sluts that loved the
Nazis!" "Don't you dare make our girls work. They're political
prisoners, they're another class from these whores around
here!"

After we had been there a week, the Russians set up a
big delousing tent near the ferry post; word was passed
around that all inmates of both the French and the General
Camp would have to pass through it. It wasn't a bad idea, but
after our experience with the medical examination we were
loath to subject ourselves to another Russian mass treatment.
We were often bothered by bedbugs and fleas at night, but we
kept our clothes and bodies as clean as possible and, as both
the skippers and the Northerners swept and scrubbed their

rooms regularly, none of us had any lice, although they abounded in the dirtier parts of the camp. Again the skippers took charge. "Don't you go there till we have investigated," they warned us.

They let the first morning go by and listened to the tales of the Belgians and Italians who had been there. They then drew straws among themselves to see which of them would do the investigating. Pete, the carpenter, and Dirk, one of the barge-hands, were so designated and were given a minimum of the oldest clothes of the whole room, for the tales of the morning had already made it clear that the treatment was ruinous on clothes. They returned late in the afternoon and turned thumbs down on the whole procedure.

"They take your clothes away and stick them into big boil-ing kettles," reported Pete, "and then you stand in line, bare-assed, till you get to the showers. There were about a dozen women in my line, and of course everybody was making passes at them. That's no place for our girls."

"And there are about ten Russian soldiers who keep order and prod you into the showers," added Dirk. "The showers are lukewarm and there is no soap. Then you have to stand in line again to get your clothes back and it takes a long time because they are all mixed up. I saw a soldier take a naked woman out of the line right behind me and disappear under the canvas of the tent. What's more, I never could find my shirt again, and look at my pants!" His trousers had shrunk to the size of jeans. Pete had come out with his shirt and trousers, but both were considerably smaller than before.

Yet, at times, the skippers' protectiveness became a problem. For example, the best time to steal vegetables was at dusk, when farmers and their families had retired indoors and one could be fairly sure that nobody would be working in the vegetable gardens close to the farms. But we were approaching the summer solstice and twilight did not come till after nine o'clock. Dorus, Pops, and the other skippers had laid down the law that none of us girls was to leave the camp after the even-

ing food line. As a result I had to resort to all kinds of dodges
to avoid their supervision; whenever they caught me with some
tomatoes or carrots (as they invariably did, because their room
was the safest place to hide my treasures) they would take me
severely to task. In this particular matter, Joke and Nell would
desert me and side with the skippers, and the general argument would be: "Why run the risk? You know that every evening the Russians go out woman hunting. If you happen to run
across them, you're sure to get it. And if you get caught at a farm
where the Russians are in charge, it will be even worse."

Oddly enough, both Dries and Jos would defend me. "She
knows what she's doing," Dries said with the proprietorial air
he assumed when talking about any one of his three girls. And
Jos, in his own slow way, added, "I followed her around one
night, you know. She keeps under cover most of the time, and
she's so fast at picking out the things she wants from any garden that I didn't even know what she had till I saw it the next
day."

In private, both of them offered to go in my place, but I
would not let them. I had studied the lie of the land and knew
exactly what to get and where. And I needed the excitement
and independence of these occasional forays to offset the
dreary institutional feeling of life in the camp, just as much as
I needed the vitamins of a few fresh vegetables.

In the evenings the camp would look even more like a gypsy
fair than during the day. While twilight lingered, there would
be tug-of-war contests on the scuffed soccer fields between the
barracks. More often than not the rope would break under the
strain of pulling, and the dozen or so men on both sides would
collapse in a flailing jumble of arms and legs. These rope-
pulling contests were especially popular among the Belgians
and Italians; as long as the rope lasted, they would go at it
again and again, each time taking a man off each team, until at
the very end there were two exhausted, snarling opponents
wearily trying to pull each other over an imaginary line that
was jealously guarded by a representative of each side. Five

or six of these contests would be going on simultaneously, each with its own little cluster of onlookers.

Others would prefer a less strenuous way of having fun. One team of three men pretending to be bear leaders appeared night after night. One man had an elaborate costume of straw and represented the bear. He walked doggedly on all fours until he got a command from his master, who led him around on a chain, to "stand up and dance". Then he would go into a frenzied dance which seemed designed to knock down as many bystanders as possible. The third man would go around with a tin cup and ask for contributions. Strangely enough, he would actually get some, even from the people who had been knocked over by the bear and were still busily dusting themselves off. One evening I looked into the tin cup—which actually was a Russian mess kit—and saw a few German marks, a couple of ruble notes, and a carefully tied package of cigarette papers.

Towards dark, when everybody was weary of fun and games, an Italian band would strike up on one of the soccer fields. It consisted entirely of violins, mandolins, and guitars; it played mostly tangos, arias from various operas, and sentimental Italian songs, and it was tremendously popular. In addition to the large audience that would gather around in ever-widening circles, it almost always commanded a small dancing space where one or two couples would give the most outrageous performances of the tango and be applauded by all onlookers.

Meantime the big mess hall was taken over by a Dutch and a Belgian band, who played alternately. The Belgians were addicted to marches, old-fashioned polkas, and popular songs. The Dutch, who had somehow managed to transport their big drums and all their other instruments from Berlin on little wagons, played nothing but jazz. There was dancing to both bands—but with a difference. As there was only about one woman to every twelve men in the camp, the Belgian, Italian, and Greek men thought nothing of dancing with each other, but the boys of the Dutch band wouldn't stand for this. Whenever they were playing, they had two strapping·giants standing on the podium with them, and the moment these two saw a couple of men dancing, they would jump down on top of them and separate them by force. The Belgians and Italians never understood what this rule was all about, but after a few scuffles they gave in and abided by it. Consequently, when the Dutch band was playing, women were in great demand, and if we happened to come in at that time, we were certain to be pounced upon and dragged into a dance before we could take a breath. For Nell, whose leg was too painful for dancing, this became so dangerous that she took to walking with a cane to make her condition clear to any would-be partners. If they still persisted, she simply used the cane to ward them off.

We dropped in almost every night, but never stayed very long, for the continuous dancing was exhausting and the messhall became unbearably hot from the animal heat of the crowd. Then, as we came out into the clear, starlit night, we would invariably be greeted by the plaintive tones of an accordion. This was played by a very homesick little Russian soldier who sat on the kitchen steps every night after dark and sadly played the same tune over and over.

And as the days passed, the rumours about an imminent exchange grew thicker and thicker, but nothing happened. Dries and I had got to know our Northerners quite well, although we never became as friendly with them as with the skippers, because we never spent any time in their room during the day. We had been told about the deal they had with the skippers. They owned a big farm-wagon with which they had arrived at the camp, but they had not seen their way clear to feeding their horse. So the skippers had taken over the care of the horse on condition that the wagon would carry their belongings whenever the transport got under way. The wagon was now being used by four Belgians, who slept underneath it and had sworn that they would let nobody steal it. The horse, during the daytime was usually tethered somewhere on the edge of the wheat or rye fields where it could nibble away at its leisure and where the skippers came several times a day to feed it whatever they had obtained for it and to make sure that it was still there. But at nightfall they would bring it around and tie it to the open window of the skippers' room, where any potential thief was sure to wake up the four men who slept next to the window.

On the tenth day of our stay in the camp the Greeks, the Yugoslavs, and a big contingent of Italians left. The skippers had put a guard on the horse from early morning and the Northerners were taking turns sitting on their wagon till, by two o'clock, the last of the "departees" had gone. Dries and I, standing at the side of the road, watched the long pathetic column of overloaded wagons drawn by very thin mules and horses, people on foot with bundles on their backs, people pulling little carts, and a few lucky ones riding or pushing bicycles from which hung all kinds and shapes of packages and cartons, as they filed out of the camp and down the hill. We had no desire to join them, for we knew they were going south-east in the direction of Wittenberg and, presumably, south from there. We just wondered how long it would take these hapless fellows to reach their destinations; some of them would have to cross three or four countries to get to their homelands. After their departure the camp was a little less crowded, the food lines were shorter, there was more room around the outdoor stoves, and the rather suspicious characters who had volunteered with the Russians to be "camp leaders" (among them the Dutch boy who wore Storm Trooper breeches and boots and whom Nell and I distrusted from the very first day) redoubled their running around with the so-called "transport lists", which never seemed to be complete and apparently had to be rechecked again and again.

Nell's leg was getting worse; we had started to worry about how we would get her out if she couldn't walk. Much as the skippers loved us, they could not promise her any room on the farm-wagon, for both they and the Northerners had considerable luggage; with twenty-six men for one big flat wagon, they weren't even sure there would be room for anybody to ride on it. "If we get a small wagon for Nell alone, do you think we could tie it to the back of your big one?" asked Joke timidly. Dorus, who, like everybody else, could not resist Joke's brand of half-childish, half-grave entreaty, said, "You just find a light little thing for the Baron here to sit in, and I promise you we'll let our horse draw it, even if all of us have to walk ourselves! Right, you fellows?" He drew a chorus of ayes from the whole room, and the search was on for a conveyance for Nell.

We found it the next afternoon in a strange, roundabout way. Jos and I were watching a boxing match between a Belgian and a Hollander. These boxing matches took place whenever people grew tired of soccer and no teams could be rounded up. The boxers went through their agreed number of rounds just for the love of the sport, but the spectators added to the excitement with the oddest kind of betting I have ever seen. The Russian soldiers loved boxing; all those who were off guard duty would join the crowd around the improvised ring. Once, right in front of me, I saw a three-way bet being made between a Russian soldier holding a fistful of roubles, an Italian who proffered about a dozen big tobacco-leaves, and a Belgian with a bundle of German marks. The three had no common language and they made their bets with nods and signs. I was glad to see that the Italian won, for right then and there tobacco was far more valuable than either marks or roubles.

On this particular afternoon Jos and I were smiling at a bet between two Belgians, consisting of three potatoes against a fairly big parsnip, when I heard a soft voice behind me calling, "Miss Roosenburg." I froze instantly. It was a long time since I had heard my last name. During the years of resistance I had been "Michèle" in France and Switzerland, "Gaby" in Belgium, and "Ann" in Holland. During my imprisonment I had been a number to my jailers and "Zip" to my cellmates. Who could possibly be calling me Roosenburg? I glanced up at Jos, but he was watching the fight and the betting and obviously hadn't heard. I wasn't sure I had heard myself, but then the voice came again, more insistent: "Miss Roosenburg!"

This time I whirled round, determined to lay this ghost—and instantly recognised the flower vendor who used to stand at the corner of my own street in The Hague and who had frequently offered me a free gift of a tired tulip, a jonquil, or a rose, from the time I was a small kid trudging home from grammar school. "Mr Vogel!——" I faltered. "How is it you're here?"

He stretched out his hand and led me away from the crowd to where we could sit down quietly with our backs to the wall of a barracks. "Gave you a start, didn't I?" he said, and smiled.

I looked at him closely. He was at least fifty-five years old—and therefore out of the range of slave labour—and he didn't have his false teeth, which made him look older. "How is it you are here?" I repeated dumbly.

"Well, it's like this, Miss Roosenburg," he answered. "There was one of these labour raids and my youngest son, who is twenty-two, happened to be out on the street. He ran home and the Nazis saw him going into our house and came after him. But we had a good hiding-place for him under the floor, you understand, so when they came in and couldn't find him, they took me instead." He told me this with such simple pride in his voice that my heart went out to him.

"When was this?" I said, not daring to ask anything about my own folks.

He turned his gentle face towards me. "It was last February first," he said. "You want to know about your family, don't you? Well, I saw your dad the day before I left. He looked pretty tired and thin, but he seemed all right. So does your mother. I hadn't seen your youngest sister for some time—she's working in a hospital somewhere. The other one is still at home. You know about your brother, don't you?"

I nodded. My brother was in Sachsenhausen concentration camp. "Are they still in the old house?" I asked. "The radio says there's heavy bomb damage in The Hague."

M

"Yes, they are," he answered. "The bridge over the canal is smashed and quite a number of houses in the neighbourhood are gone, but their block was all right when I left."

I calculated quickly. That was four months ago. Had my loved ones survived those last four months?

Later that day I visited the flower vendor in his barrack room to hear whatever other news he might have about my family and other people from the neighbourhood. As he introduced me to some of his roommates, I discovered that one of them was a barber; he agreed to trim my unruly mop of hair for the price of six cigarettes. We chatted as his scissors were deftly snipping away, and I happened to mention that Nell was unable to walk and that we were looking for some small wagon. A friend of the barber, who had been looking on and taking part in the conversation, thought he knew somebody who had just what he wanted. An involved bartering session followed, but in the end we swapped the Pram, the last of our uncut tobacco-leaves, and two hunks of bread for a small stake-wagon. It was a little replica of a German farm-wagon with four wooden wheels, the sides and back formed by stakes three inches apart and the bottom of solid boards. On the open front was a long handle to pull it by. The whole thing stood no higher than two feet; it was a foot and a half wide and about two and a half feet long—a perfect carriage for our Baron. Now we had what we needed and precious little else. Our own supplies were completely gone, and even the skippers were scraping the bottom of the barrel. And then finally, the great day came. It was June 6, 1945, and we had been free for exactly a month.

Chapter Eight

THE excitement started at six in the morning. Several Russian soldiers came stomping into the barracks to arouse the so-called camp leaders, and shortly afterwards these made the rounds of the rooms, their eternal lists under their arms. They announced that today was the day and we'd better get packed quickly. In a flash two of the skippers were out of the window untying the horse. Dries and I were still asleep in the Northerners' room, which the camp leaders had not yet reached, when our two friends appeared at the window, shoved the horse's head in, and yelled, "Come on, you lazybones, get moving or we'll leave you behind!"

Great confusion followed. Blankets came flying down from top bunks, and everybody bumped into everybody else. Dries and I wrapped ourselves in our blankets and got out of the way. In the skippers' room the same joyful bedlam was under way. Our luggage was no problem. We were all packed and ready, quietly sitting on Joke's bunk while the skippers were still feverishly working. Finally the horse and wagon, loaded with the Northerners' luggage, drew up at the window; one by one the various duffel bags and suitcases were passed through the window and added to the pile on the wagon, which was then securely tied down with long ropes and complicated skippers' knots.

At nine-thirty the kitchen bell started ringing, which meant that there was going to be a welcome food distribution. We

179

split up in two groups; one group took the first turn in the food
line while the other guarded the luggage till the first was back
to keep an eye on it. It was a good precaution, for while the
second group was gone, agonised shouts arose from a room
farther down the corridor where a group of Belgians, who had
rushed out all together at the first sound of the kitchen bell,
discovered that half of their belongings had disappeared.

We were given a full quart of soup and a half-pound hunk
of bread. We ate the soup, but stuffed all the bread in the rucksack with the saucepan and the canteen, for the very fact of
being given double portions that morning made it clear that
there would be no more food during the day. The camp leaders
made a desperate attempt to get everybody lined up in alpha-
betical squares, like luggage at the arrival of a passenger liner,
but as nobody had the slightest intention of leaving his particular group of friends, the effort got nowhere, and after an hour
of trying they gave it up.

For three hours we stood there in the hot sun, waiting and
cursing, not daring to leave and rest in the shade somewhere
for fear the column would get under way without us. Those
who had to go to the latrines stationed friends outside to shout
a warning at them if things got moving. Three times I hurried
to the washroom to have a drink and refill our canteen with
fresh water, and each time I returned panting, afraid that I
would have lost my friends in a sudden spasmodic emptying of
the camp. It was two in the afternoon before a hum of excitement buzzed through the crowd, signifying the departure of
the head of the column, and it was nearly an hour later when
the slow ripple reached our group and the good old grey horse,
who had fallen asleep between the poles, was rudely prodded
awake by one of the Northerners.

And so we set off, one farm hand walking at the horse's head,
three more Northerners in the driver's seat, a handful of skippers and Northerners riding on top of the big pile of luggage,
Nell riding in her stake wagon, which we had attached to the
rear of the big wagon with our chain and padlock, and the rest

of us walking alongside, Jos and I pulling the Tank. The first
stretch went downhill from the camp to the town of Coswig,
and Joke and Dries had to hold on to the handle of Nell's
wagon to keep it from bumping into the big one. After that we
swerved to a flat road that ran due west on the north side of
the Elbe, which at this point also ran west, and Nell jogged
quietly along without any braking or pushing. Jos had found
two flat boards that were longer than the wagon itself; on these
she could stretch her legs whenever she wanted. An elderly
man dropped back from farther ahead in the column and presented Nell with a big, old-fashioned umbrella to shelter her
from the sun. She promptly opened it up—it was black with
grey designs of birds and flowers—and from there on, whenever the column slowed down, people would run up from
behind us or drop back from ahead, just to look at Nell riding
along under her big umbrella. She smiled and nodded and
waved at all the onlookers exactly like a Queen on parade,
till finally Dorus, who had been watching her for some time,
exploded: "Hey, Baron, I think I'll promote you. You're going
to be Queen Mother from here on!"

This gag, passed up and down the line, brought even more
of the curious. It was as good a distraction as any. The sun was
hot and the road dusty. Sometimes we would slow down to a
crawl, than suddenly pick up speed and move briskly for a
little while, only to come to a sudden halt which might last as
long as half an hour. There were all kinds of reasons for these
sudden stops: a horse drawing one of the many wagons would
stumble, somebody would faint, a wheel would come off one of
the innumerable pushcarts or pram-like conveyances that held
the luggage of most of our company. Six Russian soldiers on
bicycles accompanied us. Two rode at the head and two at the
tail; the other two cycled tirelessly up and down both sides of
the road, sometimes shouting harsh orders that nobody understood, but just as often stopping to give a helping hand with luggage that had come undone or an improvised harness that had
broken. Whenever the column became too far strung out, one

would pedal up to the head and stop all movement till the tail had caught up. But whichever one came cycling past us had a wave and a big smile for Nell, and if Dorus caught them at it, he would invariably shout—in Dutch—"Salute, you lowdown so-and-so, don't you know you're passing the Queen Mother?"

Jos, Dries, Joke, and I took turns pulling the Tank, and every once in a while one of the skippers or Northerners, who took turns riding on the wagon, would give up his turn and let one of us girls ride. But I soon found that I preferred walking to riding. My blisters had healed in the camp, and I was too restless to sit still on the wagon. Moreover, the frequent stops gave me a chance to scout around for drinking water; with one canteen for the five of us, we were thirsty most of the way. At about nine o'clock in the evening we were approaching a wood and I spotted a brook running along the edge of it. The canteen was empty as usual; I quickly got it out and followed the brook upstream to refill it with clear water. I drank leisurely and washed my face and hands; just as I rejoined my friends, the column came to a sudden stop. After a while word was passed back: "We've got to get off the road; there are some Russian tanks that want to get through. We'll spend the night here."

We had learned the gypsy life all right! In about twenty minutes that whole column of about fifteen hundred people had cleared the road and spread out through the sparsely growing woods, and when, a little later, we heard the tanks rumbling by, hundreds of small cooking-fires were already winking at the first stars in the velvety June sky. Each fire had its own group of shadowy figures around it, cooking, warming themselves, making camp.

Because Nell's leg was paining, we had not moved far from the road. The skippers and the Northerners were spread in a rough half-circle somewhat deeper into the woods; between us the horse and wagon were securely tied to a tree. One of the Northerners came round with a pail. "Just give us a small piece of bread for the horse," he said. "We cut some grass and rye for him on the way and we've got some carrots. But he needs a good meal now and another in the morning. That's a pretty heavy load he's pulling, so we figured we'd all give him some bread." We cut off half of one of our half-pound chunks and dropped it in the pail. That left us two and a quarter pounds for the five of us. We decided to have a quarter-pound each and then divide up the remaining pound in the morning. Our canteen held about two quarts of water. We carefully poured out half of it in our saucepan, added half of our tea-leaves, and brewed some strong tea over our fire. Then we banked our fire, spread out our tarpaulin and canvas, and curled up close to each other, hungry, but happy in the knowledge that at least we were moving again and getting closer to our homes.

At dawn the fires blossomed out again as one group after another came awake. Pretty soon the five of us, shivering a little with the early morning cold, were warming our hands around a friendly little blaze and eating our meagre breakfast of tea and a small piece of bread. Slowly the crowd started to trickle back towards the road, and a little after seven the column started to move again. The movement was somewhat faster than the day before, and we felt good enough to sing a few of our prison songs, to the great joy of the skippers, who loved our songs and couldn't hear them often enough. When we got tired of singing, Dorus got out his harmonica and sat on the back of the wagon, playing with gusto and making everybody laugh with the funny trills and unexpected sound effects he got out of his instrument.

Around noon we reached the outskirts of a town, and the column ground to a halt again. We were standing between a row of small houses, all of them with fairly big gardens in the back; in one of these I spotted a row of cherry-trees red with fruit. I got out our saucepan quickly, sneaked through the lane between two houses, and climbed one of the trees. Sitting comfortably on a heavy branch, I started picking cherries, alternately filling the pan and popping them into my mouth. The pan was just about full when a furious woman came rushing out of the house and started screaming at me. She stood right underneath me, a fairly young woman, her face distorted with rage. Her curses and threats about getting the Russian Kommandant were quite out of proportion to the few cherries I was taking from her bounty. She behaved exactly like one of our former prison guards, and I decided to show her that I was not a prisoner any more. I said nothing and continued eating cherries, but now I was storing the pips in my cheeks and under my tongue. When my mouth was so full of pips that I couldn't slip another cherry in, I leaned over, aimed carefully, and said, "Boo!" spitting all the cherry stones full in her face. She turned white as a sheet, gasped for breath, turned, and ran back to the house. I laughed out loud with a feeling of delicious triumph. When I had eaten all I wanted and the pan was brimful, I stuffed some more cherries into my pockets and carefully swung down from the tree. The treatment had apparently been convincing; I walked through the little lane unmolested and regaled my waiting friends with both the cherries and the story.

Finally we started to move again. This time we came to what seemed to be our temporary destination, a huge open field on the bank of the Elbe. The whole column was shunted into the field and told to wait. The two Russian soldiers who waved us in also made it clear that we could not go on with the horse and wagon and had better abandon it there. Two of the skippers sauntered over to the edge of the field; after a look at the river they returned to report, "They're probably right. Dessau is on the other side of the river and there is no bridge here. We'll probably be ferried across and there wouldn't be room for the wagon." Accordingly all the luggage was unloaded and distributed to its rightful owners and the horse got innumerable pats on its neck and kisses on its nose. We had become quite attached to it and felt bad about leaving it behind, even though we knew quite well that a new owner would soon turn up; a horse was a valuable piece of property in this early postwar world.

And now began another long wait. A sort of control post had

been set up where the road reached the river, and every single person of the whole long column had to go by it, show any credentials he might have, and explain where he came from and how he happened to have been there, where he wanted to go, and so on. It was not a bad idea, for, as Jos had suspected all along, there were some Nazis and former Storm Troopers among us. Detecting a Storm Trooper was relatively easy. The minute the people at the control post had their doubts about a man, they would ask him to take off his shirt and then would inspect his armpits, for all Storm Troopers had the initials "SS" tattooed under their arms. Weeding out convinced Nazis was harder, and judging the cases of workers who had voluntarily gone to work for the Nazis was harder still—some might have done so out of genuine hardship, others out of admiration for Hitler, and some of the women simply to stay near their men. But the men at the control post did their best and, necessarily, the pace was slow.

For four hours we lay there in the grass, our heads in the shade of Nell's umbrella, dozing some of the time, daydreaming aloud most of the time. We were hungry, dirty, and impatient, and we kept up each other's spirits with extravagant visions of the service we would get once we were on the American side. Nell decided that we could abandon her stakewagon.

"But what if we have to walk on the other side?" protested Joke. "It's small enough to go on the ferry; let's take it along to be sure."

"We won't have to walk," said Nell determinedly. "Americans never walk and they won't make us do it. And you know I can manage short distances."

"What we need," mused Dries, gazing up at the shimmering sky, "is an aeroplane."

Both Jos and I sat up at this completely new idea. Till then we had been dreaming strictly in terms of trucks, buses, or trains. "Well, why *wouldn't* they move us by plane?" I said. "The Americans have millions of planes. They use them to carry troops from one place to another; they might easily have some spare ones for us."

"You forget that we're not the only ones, Zippie," sighed Jos, lying down again. "There must be millions of us all over Germany."

At last it was our turn. We let the skippers and the Northerners go first, because they had identification papers, work books, and other means of proving their stories, while we had nothing except the worn-out slip of paper from the Russian Kommandant in Riesa. Jos, out of habit and loyalty, stuck with us. The control post consisted of a small table in the shade of a big tree, and four kitchen-chairs, on which were seated, rather to our surprise, one Dutch infantry captain, one Belgian captain, an American first sergeant, and the only one of our Russian guards who spoke some German. Behind the tree stood a dejected group of about twenty people guarded by two more Russian soldiers, one with a tommy gun. They were the ones who had been weighed and found wanting. Among them, giving Nell and me a strong "I told you so" feeling, was the arrogant Dutch boy in Storm Trooper breeches who had made such a show of being a camp leader.

The skippers and the Northerners filed through easily. Then we pushed Jos ahead and he passed in a breeze. Next Nell hobbled up to the table and again acted as our spokesman. The Dutch captain looked up in surprise, "Politicals, eh?" he commented. "There aren't many in this crowd. How did you get here from Waldheim? That's quite a way south." While Nell answered, I took our Russian passport from my pocket and wordlessly showed it to the Russian soldier. He read it, laughed, and started whispering to the Belgian captain, who in turn whispered to the Dutchman on his side. Then the Dutchman passed the story on to the American, who up to that point had looked bored but now showed a sudden smiling interest. The joke escaped us, for we didn't see what was so funny about us, but when all four of them rose and shook our hands and wished us good luck, we were so gratified that we forgot to inquire about the reason for the laughter. Maybe it was the odd command of our passport.

We hurried to the ferry, Jos carrying the Tank in a fond embrace and Dries and I with the two other rucksacks on our backs. We were promptly ferried over to the other side. Nell had been right: no walking required; three trucks were waiting on the other bank. The first two were already loaded with our friends the skippers and the Northerners, and it took only the time for the next ferry to come across before our truck was filled too. Dorus, who was standing on the first truck, managed to shout at us, "So you were legitimate after all—I always had my doubts!" To which Dries yelled back, "You had better stop insulting us, or we'll tell all your stories to your wife!" Then the trucks pulled out, and between the roar of the motors and the hair-raising driving of the Negro chauffeurs, we had no more time for bantering. We just hung on for dear life, until, ten minutes later, we were deposited on a huge concrete apron in front of an impressive-looking building which still carried the legend "Eastern Command of the Luftwaffe." We were lined up there. After we had waited for half an hour and four more truckloads had been discharged, a couple of sergeants arrived, and, passing up and down in front of the ranks, asked in English and then in German if there were any political ex-prisoners among us. We stepped forward, dragging modest Jos with us, and, to our surprise, saw eleven other men come out of the ranks. "All right," announced one of the sergeant, "we'll take care of you first. Follow me."

Our feelings at that moment were quite contradictory. We were proud to be recognised as "politicals"; yet at the same time we felt a sharp regret at being thus arbitrarily separated from the skippers and the Northerners, who had given us so much friendship, help, and protection. But they themselves helped us over it by giving us a rousing cheer. There was no jealousy in the way they waved and shouted at us, nor the slightest resentment about the fact that from here on, apparently, we would be treated as different categories.

As we passed the packed ranks, I anxiously scanned the mass of faces till I saw my friend the flower vendor. He, too, waved at us cheerfully and yelled, "Good luck, hope you get home soon!"

I shouted back, "If I get there first, I'll tell your wife you're okay."

After this, things started to happen to us in fast and orderly fashion. First we were taken to the showers and for about fifteen minutes were allowed to luxuriate under hot running water in private stalls. Next we filed past two Red Cross girls who sprayed our clothes, inside and outside, with DDT—a method of delousing vastly preferable to the Russian one. Then we were led into a vast mess hall and sat down around little tables while other girls in uniform served us a meal of stew and rolls. We looked at each other unbelievingly, and I actually felt slightly uncomfortable about all this service, although Nell was visibly cheered by it and obviously felt that she had finally come into her own.

After we had wolfed down the meal, one of the Red Cross girls led us through the camp, which was so big and consisted of so many solid masonry buildings connected by trim, grass-lined walks, that we became convinced we would have a very difficult time if we ever wanted to find the skippers again. At one point we passed a field where long silent rows of Russian ex-slave labourers were squatted down, obviously waiting for something. There were about an equal number of men and women, some of the women quite young but with deeply lined faces under their babushkas. "Those are the people we exchanged you for," remarked the Red Cross girl airily. "They're waiting till we've got your whole convoy here and then they'll leave in the other direction." I looked into some of the faces that were blankly staring up at us and wondered what they were going home to.

The room assigned to us sixteen politicals was fairly large, but its only furniture consisted of a table, four iron bedsteads —only one of them with a mattress—and a pile of straw. While

we arranged ourselves and our belongings around the room (by
common consent among the men each of us girls was given a
bed, and the men spread out the straw along one wall) we
learned each other's names and snatches of each other's stories.

One of our new roommates remarked on the sad state of my
slacks. They had been badly stained when I distributed boiled
pork in Waldheim, and there were now numerous rents along
the legs and one in the seat. "I've got an extra pair of slacks I
picked up in Coswig," he said. "You can have them if you
want them."

"I don't have anything to swap for them," I said hesitantly,
looking at the bushy-haired fellow who was making the offer.
But already he was rummaging in his gear and soon he produced a perfectly serviceable pair of brown tweed man's
trousers. They fitted me fine. "You're sure you don't want anything?" I asked.

"Oh, no," he laughed, "I didn't pay for them and I don't
need them. What I really wanted was a good German camera,
so a couple of us forced our way into a German house and
threatened to rob the owners if they didn't tell us where the
biggest Nazi in town lived. Well, naturally, they gave us the
name and address, and when we went there we found the
house empty and all shuttered up. The Nazi had fled or been
arrested, I don't know which. We broke in from the rear and
found that, although the Russkis had already passed through,
there was a lot of good stuff left. I got myself a peach of a
Leica camera, and these trousers I just picked up because they
happened to be lying around."

While we were still busy installing ourselves and getting
acquainted, an army captain in Dutch uniform entered the
room and was immediately surrounded by all of us. In the first
five minutes so many questions were thrown at him that he
couldn't make himself heard, much less answer. But gradually
we quietened down. He sat on one of the beds and began to
write our names on a yellow pad of paper that he had held
under his arm. His Dutch uniform inspired enough confidence

and we gave our names and home towns readily. Then he questioned each of us briefly about what we had done during the war years and where we had been imprisoned. It was a very sketchy examination; I felt decidedly sorry that Dorus and the other skippers hadn't passed themselves off as politicals too. With Dorus's fertile imagination a good enough story for each of them would have been thought up within seconds. As the captain seemed satisfied with our case histories, we started clamouring all over again, "When can we go home?"

He shook his head sadly and said, "I can't really tell you for certain. Trains are very few and uncertain. It'll be at least two weeks before we can move you from here, and even then you'll probably go in several stages. Things are still pretty bad in Holland—all the railway men there went on strike against the Germans about ten months ago, and there's hardly been any train service since. The Germans took a lot of the rolling stock and now of course the Dutch railways are having a hard time getting organised again."

"How about flying us home?" asked Dries boldly. "They were flying Tommies home from a POW camp near Riesa."

"Yes, I know," sighed the captain, "and the French and Belgian politicals are flown home also, but it doesn't work for the Dutch."

"Why in hell not?" came the indignant question from all sides. "They aren't any better than we, are they?"

"I don't know," the captain shrugged wearily. "There probably is some sound reason for it, but I don't know what it is, I honestly don't. Believe me. I'd like to get you all home tomorrow if I could, but don't forget that there are millions of prisoners and slave labourers all over Germany, and it takes time to move so many people."

An idea was simmering in the back of my mind. "Tell me," I asked, "if French or Belgian politicals come through this camp, how do you send them to an airfield from where they can be flown home? This is obviously a big Luftwaffe headquarters; is there an airfield right here?"

"There was," he replied, "but it isn't usable now. We send them all to the big Halle airfield, which the Americans have in perfect running shape by now. All the supplies for this camp come from Halle airfield, so there's always empty trucks going back there and we have no transportation trouble."

He then launched into an explanation of the rules of the camp, but I listened with only half an ear, for my idea was taking shape. When he was preparing to leave us, I realised that there was only one thing I desperately needed to know before I could discuss the plan with my friends. At the same time I knew that this Dutch officer, if he got wind of it, would be duty-bound to stop it. So I waited till he was actually walking away, then nonchalantly fell in step with him and asked, "By the way, is there any objection here against our setting out west under our own power, same way we arrived here?"

He looked at me fully for the first time and smiled. "In a hurry, aren't you?" he said softly.

I looked right back into his eyes and continued in the same half-interested tone, "Certainly we are; we'd like to get home as fast as possible."

The captain was about my age, or maybe a year older. But, as he had told us, he had joined the Dutch Army in Britain, where he happened to be at the outbreak of the War. He had not learned the art of deception as well as we had in our five-year struggle with the Gestapo, and, even while I was using him for a plan that he could not officially approve of, I felt immeasurably older than he was and sad about this lately acquired power. The captain was scratching his head and saying slowly, "No, you are free now and we have no intention of stopping you if you want to leave. But I wouldn't advise it. It would probably take you even longer to get home. As far as I know, three parties have tried it on their own. Two of them were back in a couple of days. We don't know what happened to the third one. Maybe they were lucky and got a lift on a truck convoy going west, maybe they're just in the next DP camp."

We were at the door now and he seemed in a hurry, so I didn't press the point. "Could I talk it over in your office later this evening?" I asked politely.

"Certainly," he answered, "I'll be back there in about an hour. Now I've got to go over and see if the rest of your convoy has been taken care of and whether there are any more politicals."

My friends had already formed a huddle on one of the beds. They knew me too well to be fooled by my innocent questions and they had a pretty good idea of what I was up to. "Do you think we could manage to get on one of those evacuation planes, Zip?" asked Joke.

"With a little luck, I don't see why not," I said. "If there are empty trucks going that way all the time, it shouldn't be hard to get a ride to Halle. Once we're next to the airfield, I bet we can get on a plane. We can always pretend that we're French or Belgian."

"I don't speak French," protested Dries.

"Neither do I," grinned Jos, but he had a dancing light in his eyes, and I knew that he would pass himself off as a Turk if need be.

I looked anxiously at Nell. If she was opposed, the whole plan would fall through, for with her painful, swollen leg she was entitled to every consideration she asked for. But Nell had been quietly smiling to herself, and now said, "I'm all for it, Zip, and I must say you worked fast on that one. I'm used to organising, but I certainly didn't grasp this situation as quickly as you did. If you can't find a job in Holland, come to me and I'll get you one with the boy scouts."

This, from Nell, was the highest praise, for her boy scouts were sacred to her. But I remembered the queer, bitter feeling I had while I was drawing the well-meaning captain into my little trap, so I said half-seriously, "No thanks, I lie too much, and my good deeds come only about once a year."

I explained that we would need some proof that we really were political ex-prisoners. This captain was apparently satisfied that we were, so he could draw up a paper for us. It had to be vague about nationality though, because they might refuse us at the airfield if it said in so many words that we were Hollanders. I thought, too, that it would be better if we got our eleven companions in on the plan. A group of sixteen would make more impression at an airfield than a group of five, and the captain might not be suspicious if we asked for some kind of identification that would apply to all of us. I said to Dries, "Now, you go and tell these men about it and convince them it's our best chance. Show them your map, so they can tell Halle is south-west of here, and that if we get stuck there, we aren't any farther away from home than in this place, and that we'll have a better chance at plane transportation."

Dries, Nell, and Joke went over to the other side of the room where our new friends were loafing and chatting among themselves. But when I lay back on the bed to clarify in my own mind exactly what kind of document I wanted, Jos pushed me over to one side and lay down beside me. "I'm not much good at talking, Zippie," he said, "but maybe I can help you think."

For a while we lay there quietly, while our friends were having a lively argument at the other end of the room. I was formulating the document I wanted in my mind and Jos was stretched out beside me. Then, quite suddenly and just when I had decided on the text I wanted, I became aware of the fact that Jos was a strong virile man, who during his four months of slave labour had not suffered the same privations that we had and therefore was much more of a whole person than we were. Faintly, but unmistakably, I felt certain stirrings in my own body. On a sudden impulse I reached over, pulled his head towards me, and kissed him passionately till he roughly pushed me away.

Blushing deeply under his tan, he said hoarsely, "You shouldn't do that, Zippie. You know I have a girl back home. And there's all these people around us!"

Very contritely I answered, "I'm sorry Jos, I didn't really

N

mean to. It's just that all at once I felt like a woman again instead of like—well, like a walking mechanism. But you must understand, it's so long since I felt this way."

Jos understood, all right. He gave me a big bear hug, and when Dries and the two girls returned from their caucus to report that everybody was agreeable to our plan, we were stretched out peacefully again. I felt only slightly ashamed and mostly elated, and was all set to go to the Dutch captain's office. But Nell wisely advised caution. "If we're too eager, he might suspect something," she said. "Wait a little longer."

We waited till almost 8 p.m.; then Dries and I and two representatives from our new friends went over to the captain's office. We had decided beforehand that I would be spokesman, but that if I got into trouble, the others would take over in turns. But it was all ridiculously easy. I explained that we had no papers and that, if from here on we wanted to travel as a group, whether we stayed at the camp or left on our own, we needed some document to show that we were politicals.

"What do you have in mind?" the captain asked. He swivelled round to his ancient typewriter, and I practically dictated the document he typed out for us in duplicate. It ran something like this: "To whom it may concern: The following persons are all political ex-prisoners who crossed the Russian-American lines at Coswig/Dessau. They are to be accorded priority on all kinds of transportation to France, Belgium, and Holland, from wherever they request transportation."

There followed our sixteen names and the signature of the Dutch captain, plus some important-looking stamps. He gave us one copy of this document and kept the other one for himself. As I had been the safekeeper of the Russian passport, I automatically became the keeper of this new one, which I folded away carefully in one pocket of my newly acquired trousers. I knew it was just what we needed: the document did not mention our nationality or the kind of transportation we were entitled to, and gave us leeway to make use of almost anything that came our way.

Exultant, the four of us returned to our room and announced our triumph. Among the sixteen it was quickly decided that, if we had to, we would all pretend to be Belgians and the eight who did not speak French would simply pass as Flemish. After some discussion, we also agreed to start out the next morning. Some of the men would have liked to rest a little and have a chance at three meals a day. But we stood firm. It was now or never. If we stayed, the captain might have second thoughts and recall our precious document.

At last the room grew silent; as I settled myself comfortably on the steel springs of my bed, I wondered sleepily whether the captain had really been taken in or whether this had been his way of giving us a chance that he could not officially allow. Rather regretfully, I decided that the former was more probably true, for he had signed his name and rank and used official stamps, which he would have tried to avoid if he were playing our game. But my conscience wasn't strong enough to keep me awake. I turned over, and in a few minutes was sound asleep.

At eight the next morning all sixteen of us filed into the mess hall. We had our belongings packed and were ready to move, but a free breakfast before setting out was not a thing to be scorned. Expectantly we sat down at the tables and, still to our surprise, the waitresses appeared again and served us scrambled eggs, bread, and big mugs of steaming coffee. We grinned at each other over these incredible riches, but when one of the men suggested again that we might stay a few days and take advantage of this food, we finished our breakfast quickly and got up to go.

"Come on, you chaps," said Nell in her most compelling tone, "we've got things to do today!" With that she hobbled out, never even looking back, and the whole crowd followed obediently. We picked up our luggage and quietly found our way to the exit from the camp and from there to a road where a big sign pointed to Berlin in one direction and to Halle in the other. There we waited patiently for about half an hour, till finally a big truck came thundering along in the right direction.

We waved and shouted, and it screeched to a stop. An amiably grinning Negro poked his head out of the cab and asked where we wanted to go. "Halle airfield," we yelled, and he said, "That's where I'm going, hop aboard."

He got down from the cab—a tall, coal-black man, looking enviably clean and trim in his well-fitting uniform—and opened the tailboard of the truck. While he helped us climb aboard he noticed our Tank, which we had brought along, half out of sentimentality, half because we didn't know where we were going and might still need it. He went into a paroxism of laughter, slapping his thigh and shouting, "What you need that thing for? That ain't going to get you nowhere fast!"

We laughed with him, but nevertheless shoved our tiny Tank onto the big American truck before we climbed on ourselves. Then he fastened the tailboard behind us and we were off on another hair-raising ride. The towns and villages in that part of Germany, as in most of Europe, have narrow, crooked streets, but this didn't bother our driver. He turned round corners of cobblestoned streets as if he wanted to scrape the dirt off the plaster of the houses, and barrelled through church squares as if they were national highways. But he didn't hit anything, and we covered the distance between the DP camp and the airfield —a little over thirty miles—in twenty-five minutes.

Just before we arrived at the airfield we passed a big DP camp of tents and barracks and for a moment I was afraid he was going to deposit us there. But he whisked right past it and didn't stop the truck till we were well inside the grounds and right in front of the office of the commanding officer. As we climbed down, still slightly dazed from the fast ride, I asked our grinning driver, "What's that big camp we just passed?"

"Oh, them's French and so on," he answered casually. "They're waiting to be flown out of here. You all aren't French, are you?"

"No," I answered gravely, "We're Australians."

It was a poor joke, but he was still laughing at it after we had all pumped his hand and thanked him for the ride. We had a quick consultation among ourselves and decided that the same delegation that had obtained the letter from the Dutch captain would tackle the American commander of this airfield. The others waited outside while the four of us, rather timidly, filed into the ramshackle building that was marked as the command post.

Inside we found a young and visibly harassed man sitting behind a desk with several telephones. "Now, who the hell are you?" he barked at us.

I didn't know how to address him, for he wore only Air Force trousers and shirt; and his coat was nowhere in sight, so I couldn't tell his rank. He might be a corporal or a colonel. "We're political ex-prisoners, sir," I started politely, taking our document out of my pocket and putting it in front of him; then, as I saw a frown come over his face, I continued hastily "and we have priority on transportation because we were condemned to death. Could we get a plane from here?"

I was lying again, for the fact that Dries, Joke, Nell and I had actually been condemned to death had nothing whatsoever to do with our phony priority. But I wanted to get home, and I told myself quickly that I was entitled to use this dreadful phrase if, for once, it could help us. It did have its effect. The face of the young man in front of us changed and his voice was softer when he asked, "Condemned to death, eh? Well, you're lucky you escaped. How many of you are there?"

"We're sixteen, sir," Dries replied quickly. "The others are waiting outside."

"Sixteen," he said to himself, scanning our document, and then to us, "I've got a plane leaving for Brussels in twenty minutes. I could put you on that one. Is Brussels all right with you?"

This time we answered in chorus, "Yes, sir!" and, while he handed our letter back to me, he barked a command into an adjoining room. A corporal scurried into sight. "Take these people to that C-47 that's taking off for Brussels," ordered our benefactor, "and be sure they don't take too much luggage aboard. Get a move on!"

We couldn't believe it, but the corporal hustled us out of the room before we could properly say "Thank you." And the young man behind the desk seemed to have forgotten about us already—he was barking orders into the phone.

Once outside, remembering the admonition about not much luggage, we untied our rucksacks from the Tank and parked it neatly in a corner where it wouldn't be in the way. Like the skippers and their horse, we had become quite attached to our little wagon and would have liked to carry it home as a souvenir. But our Negro driver had been right: it wouldn't get us anywhere fast, and we suddenly seemed to have picked up a speed far beyond our fondest hopes.

Half an hour later we were airborne.

In the plane, which we shared with a dozen American soldiers, we huddled closely together in our bucket seats and kept pinching each other to make sure that it was all true. Now we were winging our way towards the country where we belonged. Never mind if we landed in Belgium or France, instead of Holland. Once there, the road home wouldn't be so arduous, for we would be surrounded by people who understood our plight. Once in a while we would take a look out of the small windows at Germany, land of unhappy memories. But, quite appropriately, Germany was shrouded by grey and ragged rain clouds that left only patches of land visible here and there, and our only feeling about any such patch of land was that we wanted to get away from it as quickly as possible.

These were the thoughts we all had, but we said very little. We just didn't have words big enough to describe our feelings.

Chapter Nine

THE flight lasted only about two and a half hours; about 2 p.m. we landed at an airfield outside Brussels. We were told to stay in the plane while the American soldiers and the crew got off, and I held my document at the ready. But presently a British soldier came round and politely requested us to alight and come over to the mess hall. Dumbly, we followed him through a slight drizzle into a wooden shack; immediately we were offered Spam sandwiches and big mugs of tea mixed with plenty of milk. Unobtrusively I slid our document back into my pocket. Apparently it was not required at this moment. But what were we supposed to do or to say?

None of us had the slightest clue about our next move; in our embarrassment we accepted more sandwiches and more tea, which the Tommies kept pressing on us, and most of us were in dire need of a lavatory. It was Joke who saved the situation by innocently asking, "Are we going to leave here soon or will I have time to go to the bathroom?"

Her question produced two much-needed answers: the location of the bathrooms, and the information that we were waiting for a truck to take us to a DP reception centre in Brussels. After that a lot of general information was exchanged with the Tommies. They wanted to know where we came from and why, and we wanted to know what their part in the War had been, and we happily swapped stories. "What happened to the Americans who brought us here?" I asked at one point, and

199

one of them said, with a shrug of his shoulders, "They had a truck waiting for them. We're supposed to take care of you. But don't worry, our chap will turn up soon."

Eventually he did turn up, with a covered truck just big enough to carry all of us. We climbed aboard and the truck drove off. I was quite familiar with the countryside around Brussels, but I had always seen it ahead, either on foot or on a bicycle, and the backward view, which was all that the truck afforded, confused me. However, I knew that the truck was taking much too long from an airfield to the town, and I kept looking for landmarks. After about an hour, I had seen enough of them to realise that we were driving round Brussels instead of going into the town. We hammered on the back of the cab till the British driver stopped the truck and stepped down from his cab to ask us what we wanted.

"You're lost," I said accusingly. "If you go on this way, we may come back to the airfield, but most likely you'll get tangled up in one of the suburbs on the north, and then we'll never get out!"

He admitted he was lost and got out a map. Joke and I showed him where we were, and one of our companions offered to guide him in. We reached the rue de la Régence; from there our Tommy knew his way, and he brought us straight to the DP reception centre.

This proved to be a roomy house fitted for about sixty people. Downstairs were a big dining-room (it couldn't even be called a mess hall), an office, showers, and a big reception hall. We were quickly passed through the showers and once again "deloused" with DDT. Then all of us were given a Red Cross package which contained toothbrush, towels, soap, chocolate bars, and cigarettes. Having been so well fed at the airfield, some of our group actually tried to refuse these packages. But the good ladies who were doing this work voluntarily wouldn't hear of such a thing. "Take it, take it," they urged. "You may not need it now, but you may later. Holland has only just been liberated. They aren't so well off as we are."

Next we were led upstairs; our company was divided over several rooms which had eight bunks each. As usual, the five of us stuck together and were assigned to the same room, which we shared with a Jewish couple and their eight-year-old daughter who had somehow escaped from the horrible Belsen concentration camp. The bright elderly lady who had conducted us to our quarters stood in the doorway till we had taken possession of our bunks simply by depositing our bundles at the head of the beds and introducing ourselves to the Jewish family who occupied top bunks. Then she said, rather impatiently, "Now, I'll take you downstairs and I have a real surprise for you. Come on now!"

Obediently we followed. "Now, here's the dining-room," she said expansively, showing us a well-appointed room with five tables for six. "Breakfast from seven till eight-thirty, lunch from eleven-thirty till one, and dinner from five-thirty till seven. We've set it up nicely for you, haven't we?"

It was almost too nice—we didn't quite know what to do or to say. But our lady wasn't finished. "The first shift for dinner will come on pretty soon," she said, peering at us, "but I imagine that will be filled up by the people who have been here for some time. That will give you about forty-five minutes till it's your turn. Would you like to see a little of the town? We have these for you, you know." With that she went over to a locker in the reception hall, brought out a handful of badges, and pinned one on each of us. "That'll give you free rides on buses and trams," she said with a fond laugh, "so you can ride all over town if you like. But remember, we close this house at eleven o'clock, so be sure to be back by that time or you'll have to sleep on the streets."

At last I caught my breath. I had many friends in Brussels and I wanted to get in touch with them. What's more, Nell, Joke, and I were also dying to know whether Lottie and her mother and all our various Belgian cellmates had returned to their homes. So when the lady stopped talking, I asked, quite diffidently, "I saw two telephone booths in the hall. May we use them?"

She was on her way out, having done her duty, but she stopped in her tracks and asked, "Now what do you want to do that for?"

"I've got some friends in this city," I answered falteringly, feeling like a six-year-old answering the teacher.

Immediately, she turned around, her purse already open in her hands. "You should have told me before," she said sternly, handing me the necessary franc pieces for four calls.

"Look," I said, "my friends have money—can we pay this back?" But already she had swung out of sight—she was the grand lady doing charity and she would not be bothered with the pitiful amount of four telephone coins.

I rushed to the telephone and dialled a number of my old resistance days. I was calling a well-known dealer in Chinese antiques. His wife came on the phone. "This is Gaby," I said breathlessly.

"Gaby, are you alive?" she shouted. "Where are you calling from?"

"I'm right here in Brussels?"

"Come on over, I've got something to show you."

"I will, but I've got four friends with me. Can I bring them?"

"Indeed you can, come right over."

Ignoring the dinner awaiting us, I explained quickly to my friends that we were all invited. We trooped outside and climbed onto a tram. The badges worked like a charm; people even stood up to give us their seats. And soon, as in a long-forgotten dream, I was back in the old narrow street behind the St. Gudule Cathedral, ringing the bell of the antique shop. My Belgian friend Yvonne, plump and smiling as I had always remembered her, stood at the head of the long staircase that led up to the living quarters above the shop; I couldn't climb those stairs quickly enough. In the confusion of kissing her and pumping the hands of her husband and son who were waiting in the doorway of the living-room, I almost forgot to introduce my friends. But eventually we got everything straightened out and she led us into the living-room.

"Look," she said, pointing at the table. There, neatly arranged in a ring of flowers, was a letter in my mother's handwriting. I stood looking down on it unbelievingly, unable to speak. "Go on, read it," she urged gently, and I reverently picked up the paper. It was dated May twenty-fifth. My mother had survived the War! With tears running down my face, I read the rest. It was a letter thanking my Belgian friends for a parcel of foodstuffs they had sent over immediately after Holland was liberated, and it said that the whole family, my father, mother, and two sisters were very thin and underfed but alive, but that they had no news about either me or my brother. My knees started to wobble, and I sat down abruptly.

"What is it, Zippie?" the others asked eagerly. "What does it say?"

"They're all alive," I sobbed, "my family is alive, except they haven't heard from my brother yet."

Laughing and crying in my happiness, I hugged everybody in the room. My friends shared my feelings. Even if they had no word from their families, somehow this letter seemed a good omen for all of us. And then something odd occurred to me. My Belgian friends had always known me as "Gaby" and were even now calling me that. How had they discovered my real name and my parents' address? They explained that they had remembered a phone number I often called during my irregular appearances at their house and that I spoke Dutch during those calls. On a hunch that I might have been speaking to friends who knew my real name, they had called the same number after Holland had been liberated. Their hunch had been right; they had easily obtained my name and had sent a parcel to my parents. They knew there had been a terrible famine in northern Holland, and also they wanted news about me.

It was an unforgettable evening. My Belgian friends normally spoke French, but they knew a few words of Flemish, which they threw in now and then for the benefit of Dries and Jos, who otherwise relied on our rather hectic translating.

Yvonne brought in cake and dry vermouth; while we were freely partaking of both, she told us that she, her husband, and her son, had been arrested about two weeks later than I.

"That's strange," I said, "I never gave them your name or address. And the Gestapo never questioned me about you after you were caught either."

"Yes, we know it wasn't through you," they answered. "They never connected you with us during the interrogation. We're still not sure how it came about, although we have certain suspicions."

"But when were you liberated, and where?" I asked. "You haven't just come home, have you? You don't look like it."

"You mean I've got all my weight back," laughed Yvonne. "So will you, Gaby, so will you! Here, have some more cake." It turned out that they had been held in a prison in Brussels, and then herded into a train for transport to Germany; but the Allied armies had overrun Brussels so fast that the train had not been able to leave, and they had simply walked home from the station through streets crowded with Allied soldiers and a deliriously happy population. A friend had taken care of the shop during their absence and their priceless antiques were safe.

When the first and urgent news had been exchanged, we suddenly remembered our Belgian friends from the NN group in Waldheim. Convinced that they had long since come home, we asked if we could use the telephone to call them. There was no answer to the number of Lottie and her mother, but I remembered the married name of Lottie's twin sister, found it in the directory, and got her on the phone. I don't know which of us was more surprised: she to hear a strange voice telling her that her mother and sister were alive and on their way home, or I to discover that, although they had left Waldheim five days before us and had not had to cope with the Russians, they had not yet returned. I finally hung up the phone and related to my friends what I had just heard.

"You know what, Zip," said Joke in pure amazement.

"Maybe they were stuck in that big DP camp we saw just before we came to the Halle airfield. That would be a logical place for them, coming from Altenburg."

"My God!" said Nell. "You mean to say maybe we passed right by them and got on a plane when they'd been waiting for a month?"

"And a damn' good thing we did!" said Dries. "You know perfectly well that plane would have taken off three-quarters empty if we hadn't come along. We didn't take anybody else's place!"

"In that case," resumed Nell with her usual practicality, "we must call the families of all those that were in Waldheim with us and spread the good news."

For about an hour we huddled at the phone, with Yvonne hovering around us, filling up our cake plates and vermouth glasses. We had been so convinced that the fifteen Belgians who had been NNs with us in Waldheim had returned long before us that we hadn't even brought along the list of names and addresses we had carried all the way. We remembered most of the names, however, and would read the telephone directory till we came to an address that sounded familiar. In some cases there would be no answer. In others, new tenants had moved in and did not know the address of the former occupants. But with Joke, Nell, and I taking turns at the telephone, we did manage to reach at least six families who were highly pleased to hear the news.

Yvonne got me into a corner alone and pressed a lot of small change into my hands.

"Don't do that," I protested, "we're very well taken care of. We can even ride on the trams without paying!"

"Don't make a scene," she said. "I sold a Chinese vase yesterday for more than the price my husband had put on it. And keep in touch with me, will you?"

One question had been on my mind all that evening; now I asked Yvonne, "How long do the mails take between here and Northern Holland?"

She shook her head and said, "The letter you saw this evening took ten days. I'm still surprised our parcel got through at all. If you're thinking of writing to your family, forget about it; you'll probably be home before your letter arrives. They'd rather see you in the flesh than on a piece of paper, anyway."

On the tram back to the DP centre I suddenly confided to Joke, "I've been racking my brains for about two weeks now, but I just can't remember my home telephone number. Do you remember yours?"

"Yes," she said proudly, and reeled it off, "Zeist ——." I checked all the others while we rocked along in the tram. Nell and Jos had no trouble whatsoever. Dries had to think hard before he could recollect the Arnhem telephone number of his mother, but did manage to find it in the recesses of his memory. But however hard I tried, I could not recall mine. "Why worry about it, Zippie?" said Joke, putting a comforting arm around my back. "I asked your Belgian friends about it, for I had a wild idea that maybe I could call home. But the only established lines from here go to Eindhoven, and apparently there is still no telephone contact with the northern part of Holland."

"Yes, I know," I said. "I asked them the same question. But it's just possible that doctors' phones might be in order."

"We aren't in Holland yet," Nell cut in, "and telephoning from here is impossible. We all seem to have discovered that much. Just sleep on it—maybe you'll remember tomorrow."

It was ten minutes to eleven when we rang the bell at the reception centre and a sleepy-eyed girl opened the door for us. On tiptoe, so as not to awake the Jewish family who were sound asleep, we fixed our bunks and prepared ourselves for the night. The bunks had real mattresses and even pillows. All we had to do was spread out our blankets.

We slept late the next morning and didn't turn up for breakfast till about eight. We found a table for ourselves, and again the incredible happened: waitresses brought us scrambled eggs, toast, margarine, and a big pot of coffee, with plenty of sugar and milk. We helped ourselves liberally, and as we were smoking some of the cigarettes that were given us, over our third cup of coffee, one of the waitresses came round and told us that the "political officer" was ready to see us in the office next to the dining-room.

The officer apparently wanted to see us one by one, and by sheer accident I was the last to go in. We had pushed Jos ahead of us, because he had his papers, and then Dries had helped Nell because her leg was troublesome. Joke and I were sitting in the hall when the door opened and a British corporal asked, "Next one to come up?" and I pushed Joke because I wanted to finish my cigarette.

It took Joke only five minutes; then my turn came. I found myself face to face with a Dutch colonel, whose first gesture was to offer me an English cigarette. I accepted it, sat down, and, thus at ease, was entirely unprepared for the words that burst over me. "You don't have to tell me who you are," said the colonel from behind his desk. "Your team-mates told me and I looked you up in our reports. You're all right as far as I'm concerned. But will you please explain to me why you come flying into Brussels with one Storm Trooper and one man whom I strongly suspect to be a Nazi, although I can't prove it as yet?"

I looked at him and saw a broad, generous mouth, a sharp hawk nose, and cold grey eyes behind steel-rimmed spectacles. Within three or four seconds we had sized each other up. I knew he was stronger than I and that I didn't want to wage any battle with him. I was tired of battles. He had won before we ever tangled. I took the list of names out of my pocket and handed it over to him. "That's how we did it, sir," I admitted softly. "I didn't know a damn' thing about any of those eleven names that you see below ours, except that they proclaimed themselves to be politicals. But we were told that only the Belgians and the French could fly home. I didn't think that was fair, so I talked the Dutch officer into giving us this paper. I put all sixteen names on it because I thought that would give us a better chance at a plane than a small group of five."

He was looking over my precious document and a smile was now lurking around the corners of his mouth. "It obviously did," he said dryly. "You didn't show much respect for the Dutch uniform, did you?"

That thought had never even occurred to me. "I'm not sorry I did it, sir," I said defensively. "I still don't think it's fair that we were not supposed to fly home."

"There's a very good reason for that," he answered, his voice gentle now. "In the first place, there isn't a single airfield in Holland in good enough condition to handle big planes. In the second place, Holland itself is in very bad shape. There has been a lot of destruction and a terrible famine for the last six months. We can't let thousands of you go home to a country where there still isn't enough food for the population that's already there."

"You mean we've got to stay here?" I asked, crestfallen.

He shook his head. "No, the south of Holland has been free for nine months now. They can take care of you there. We've got three reception centres here and they're all almost full. I think there'll be a train in two or three days." With that he stood up and held out his hand. The grey eyes were twinkling behind the glasses. "I suppose I should really tell you off," he said, smiling, "but to tell you the truth, I'm glad you made that plane. Just be a little more careful about your company next time you pull a stunt like that."

I rejoined my friends, who were waiting for me at one of the tables in the dining-room. "That's one hell of a fellow!" I remarked.

"We were trying to figure out who the SS man was among those others," said Dries, "but frankly, I haven't the faintest idea."

"Neither have I," I said airily, "but who cares? He got caught, didn't he?"

We decided to split up for the rest of the day. Joke had several resistance friends she wanted to look up, and so did I. Dries and Jos wanted to see the town, and I gave them most of the money Yvonne had provided me with, for I knew I wouldn't need it. The remainder went to Nell, who wanted to give her leg a rest and stay at the centre that day. To while the time away, she was going to try to make some out-of-town phone calls we had not succeeded in making the night before.

We spent three happy days in Brussels, visiting friends or just roaming around and goggling at the shop windows. Brussels was really booming then, and the shops were bursting with goods we hadn't seen for years. One day I went to see the Dutch friends who had given Yvonne my real name. They decided my return called for a real celebration and took me to the best restaurant in town. Up to that point I had not been self-conscious about my clothes, but when I entered the mirrored, softly lighted restaurant and saw the flowers and the gleaming white tablecloths, I suddenly realised that I still looked like a tramp in my frayed sweater, my man's trousers, and my heavy shoes that were one size too big. However, even here the political prisoner's badge worked wonders; the head waiter led us to the best table as if I were a princess in a resplendent evening gown.

And then I was dazedly looking at an enormous menu with a long list of dishes that sounded too good to be true. I was incapable of choosing among them till all at once I saw the words "Roast duck with oranges", and had a sudden vision of our bare, dirty cell in Waldheim on the last day of our imprisonment, when Laure had kept us spellbound with her succulent description of how to prepare that special dish. Putting the menu down, I said gravely to my host, "It'll have to be roast duck with oranges, Emile."

"You can have anything you want," he said. "Is roast duck a special favourite of yours?"

I replied, "I had a cellmate who could describe it so beautifully that you almost felt you were eating it. Now I'd like to know what it feels like when one really eats it."

It was the best meal I ever ate. My friend Emile, who was a connoisseur of food and wines, saw to it that we had the best.

o

The whole evening had a dreamlike, never-never-land quality. Only five nights ago I had been dining on a lump of sour bread and a little strong, unsugared tea in a wood along the Elbe river, without a penny in my pocket, without an established identity, without knowing whether I had a family to return to. Yet here I was dining in a first-class restaurant, with waiters hovering at my elbow, champagne flowing freely, my plate never empty, and myself blissful in the knowledge that my family was safe and that the security officer apparently knew my personal record.

When I got back to the centre that evening, a few minutes before eleven, I found Dries and Jos playing draughts in the dining-room, waiting for me. "Nell and Joke have gone to bed," Dries said. "What's the matter with you, Zippie? You look strange. Are you drunk?"

"I don't know," I said truthfully. "Maybe it's the champagne, maybe it's just being alive. You know what I feel like? I feel like one of those violinists at a concert who gets called back for an encore. I was so convinced I was going to die and that the concert was over, but apparently life wants an encore. I just realised that tonight."

Another result of my visits to various friends around Brussels was that I collected an impressive amount of tinned food, instant coffee, bags of sugar, candy bars, and so on. Every family I saw insisted on giving me something, for they knew that people still went hungry in the northern part of Holland. Joke had the same experience. I gave some of it to Dries, Nell, and Jos, for they knew nobody in Brussels and did not have the same chance of collecting food.

So, when on the morning of June twelfth, we all lined up in the reception hall to await transportation to the station where a train would take us north, I had not only a rucksack on my back but also a bulky, roughly sewn canvas bundle in my hands. There were about fifty-five of us standing in the reception hall, all packed and sacked, and I looked around the crowd to see how many of our eleven flight companions were there. To my relief I recognised the bushy-haired fellow who had given me my new trousers. In some obscure way, I was gratified to know that he wasn't the Storm Trooper whom the knowledgeable colonel had had arrested. But my memory proved faulty at this point. I could pick out most of those who had been with us during our brief association, but I couldn't remember the two faces that were missing. Neither could my friends when I asked them about it. "Who cares?" said Jos, after a brief period of studying the crowd. "Remember, Zip, we're going to play our encores now. No use looking back."

At last two British trucks drove up; we all crowded aboard and were taken to Brussels' north station, where another group of Dutchmen was already waiting. Packages of sandwiches and fruit were distributed. We had been free now for almost five weeks, and our hollow cheeks had filled out considerably. Just the day before, I had weighed myself on a scale in the house of one of my friends, and discovered that I had already regained half of the weight I had lost during the long months in prison. Then the third group of Dutchmen arrived; now we were all lined up along the platform, about one hundred and eighty strong, each with his own bundles, and his own eager hopes about a new life ahead.

Finally the train drew up at the platform, one old-fashioned locomotive pulling two wooden third-class coaches. Our train covered about seventy miles, but because of various shuntings and delays it took four hours. The mood on the train varied with its speed. When it went fast, everyone sat on the wooden benches, lost in his own dreams and reluctant to talk. When the train slowed down, everybody would crowd into the corridors that ran along the compartments, look out through the windows, and invent theories about why the train had slowed down. I was standing at the window when we passed the Roosendaal station. I happened to know that station inside out, for I had had a bicycle stored there during the War and, on moonless nights, had often used it to get across the Dutch-Belgian border, cycling along the narrow paths that belonged to the smugglers; one can find them along any guarded border.

I shouted to my friends, who were quietly sitting in the compartment, "We're in Holland now. Come and look at it!" They joined me at the window and all of a sudden, while we were looking at those flat, neatly worked fields, contrasting with many shot-up and burned-out farm-houses, something clicked in my brain. I had remembered my home phone number! Nell was standing next to me and I impetuously threw my arms around her, singing, "The Hague 114261!"

Shortly afterwards, the train pulled up at the station of the small village of Oudenbosch, and, to our surprise, we found a reception committee of joyous monks waiting for us. There were at least a dozen of them; they scurried around among us, helping us alight, accepting bundles that were passed through windows, forming us into a column, and being generally helpful to one and all. With their black robes flapping against their legs and their tonsured pates shining in the sun, they reminded me of a bunch of crows just arrived at some particularly promising feeding-ground. They had thoughtfully provided a small pushcart, meant for the transportation of mailbags, and we installed Nell in this with most of our luggage. And then the whole crowd walked off to what would be our next resting-place, a big Catholic monastery. It was a twenty-minute walk to the large, cobblestoned courtyard within the walls of the rambling buildings. There we were lined up again and more monks swarmed out to bid us welcome and tell us how happy they were that we had come home alive. During the War, I had had good contacts with two nunneries, where the intrepid sisters had even gone so far as to shelter Allied pilots (suitably disguised in nuns' garb), but I had never been in a men's monastery before. I looked around with eager interest.

"Tell me," I asked of a passing monk, "how many people can you put up here?"

"At present we have between fifteen hundred and two thousand," he replied courteously. "Two thousand is about our limit."

"But where do you put them all?" I marvelled.

He answered with a smile, "It's amazing, you know, how many people you can put up when the Lord wants you to do so. First we found that we could make a lot of room by tripling up in our cells instead of each having a cell of his own. Then we arranged those old stables that we weren't really using. The library came next. Now some of us are quartered in the town, and that makes even more room."

"It's wonderfully kind of you to be doing all this for us," Joke broke in.

The monk, who had that peculiar aura of childlike gaiety that seems to be characteristic of all the nuns and monks I have ever met, laughed out loud and retorted, "I understand you people did something for us, didn't you?" Then he grew serious again and added, "Of course our accommodation is not as good as what you had in Brussels. I understand they give you private bunks and all kinds of wonderful meals. Here you will sleep in straw and we serve two meals a day, but they're good meals."

"How long do you think it will be before we can go home?" asked Nell. "We all belong in northern Holland, you know."

All of a sudden, our monk was in a hurry. "I can't really tell you," he said, looking away. "Ask the security officers when you get around to them." With that he moved on down the line, leaving us wondering.

The line had been moving slowly but steadily, and soon afterwards it was our turn. To our great satisfaction, we were led to an office where three doctors were working overtime trying to handle the flow of newcomers. The examination was necessarily sketchy—blood-pressure, pulse, tongue and throat inspection, testing of nerve reactions, brief listing of personal complaints—but at least Nell got some medicine for her leg and, even more important, we were all passed before the fluoroscope and pronounced free of tuberculosis. This had been a secret fear for us three girls and for Dries. We had been in such close and intimate contact with tuberculosis for so many

months that we never could be sure whether we had contracted
it or not, and by now we had heard enough about the situation
in northern Holland to know that we had better stay away
from our underfed families if we had any sign of this dread
illness.

The next step in our monastery initiation was the political
security committee. They allowed us to come in as a group and
processed us in record time. I did not quite understand how
they could give us such cavalier treatment, until we were ready
to file out of the room. Then the Dutch colonel winked at me
and whispered, "I understand you had some trouble with my
colleague in Brussels!"

A monk who had been waiting at the door now led us to a
table in the next room, where tags were given out for various
room assignations. Here we finally had time to pop the big
question again, "When can we go home?"

"Oh, it'll be two or three weeks or so," answered the efficient
matronly lady who was working behind a big table, with a
crowd of monks as messenger boys. "Now, let's see, you three
girls had better go to Wing A, and as for you two young men,
you can sleep in one of the cells of our brothers here."

But Nell couldn't be put off that easily. "Why can't we go
north tomorrow?" she asked belligerently.

The lady looked up and gave her an efficient answer, "There
isn't enough food in the north," she said crisply. "We'd just
make it worse by sending you people in. Any of you live south
of the rivers?" We dumbly shook our heads. "Well, then you'll
just have to be patient," she concluded. "Now you go and find
your quarters, and if you have any complaints, report to me."

We were definitely dismissed and, in deference to the monks
in whose house we were staying, we even allowed our group to
be separated, the men going one way and the women another,
but not before we had made a quick rendezvous for half an
hour later at the portal of the courtyard.

Dries and Jos were waiting for us at the appointed time of
five o'clock. We knew that dinner was being served, but,

having munched away on our Belgian sandwiches all afternoon, we weren't hungry. Nell, feeling a lot better as a result
of the medicament she had been given for her leg, said, "Let's
make a tour of the village before we join the food line." Arm in
arm, the five of us strolled down the village street.

In the next few seconds, the miracle happened. A first
lieutenant in Dutch uniform turned a corner into the main
street. Next thing my friends knew, I had flown down the
street and was hanging around the lieutenant's neck, hugging
and kissing him and making a perfect spectacle of myself.
They stood and stared until I finally came to my senses and
introduced the lieutenant as my cousin, Dirk Roosenburg.

To the everlasting glory of my cousin, it must be said that he
recovered very quickly from my assault. "What the hell! I
thought you were dead," he said. "But as long as you aren't,
come and have dinner at the officers' mess!"

"How is it you're with the Dutch Army?" I asked, knowing
that he had played a considerable role in the resistance.

"Easy," he said, smiling. "You know we live south of the
rivers. As soon as our town was liberated I joined up."

"Are your wife and kids all right?" I asked anxiously.

He answered, "Oh yes, they're fine. The town of Eindhoven
was damaged quite a bit, but as you know we lived outside
and we didn't have any trouble. Now how about you?"

As quickly and concisely as I could, I told him our experiences.

"So you're stuck in that monastery, eh?" he said reflectively.
"It'll take three weeks to a month before they let you go north."
He thought it over for a few minutes, then said, "Is that your
group, just the five of you? Let me take you to the officers' mess
now and I'll join you later. I may cook up something for you."

We were marched to the officers' mess, which was round the
corner in the next street, and Dirk ordered the mess sergeant to
serve us drinks "within reason". We were hardly established
around the long table, carefully sipping Dutch gin and speculating what Dirk was up to, when another officer walked in,

who proved to be an old friend of mine from Leiden University. This was Holland all right—the place where you could hardly make a move without encountering a member of your family, an old school friend, or some odd acquaintance from somewhere. This very feature of Dutch life had often been an annoying hindrance during resistance days, when it frustrated all attempts at keeping one's true identity secret, but just now it was a heart-warming experience.

Dirk returned half an hour later and introduced us to the other officers who came strolling in. Then he took me into a corner and said cheerfully, "It's all arranged, kid. I've got a car and a driver who has to go north tomorrow with secret orders. You be ready at the portal of the monastery tomorrow morning at eight sharp and he will pick you up."

I said, completely flabbergasted, "You're doing a wonderful thing for us, Dirk. You sure this won't get you into trouble?"

"Never mind if it does," he laughed. "You've got a right to go home and I'm going to get you there. There's only one thing—that driver has to be back here by night and you have to make a big detour, for there is only one place where the rivers can be crossed, above 's Hertogenbosch, all the other bridges are out. He probably will not have time to drop all of you in your home towns."

I couldn't believe my ears; neither could my friends when I passed on the good news. We had a hilariously happy meal, topped off with big dishes of strawberries which the orderlies brought in as a special treat for us from the officers whose table we were sharing. Then we returned to the monastery, fairly bursting with our tremendous news, which we knew we had to keep strictly to ourselves.

None of us slept much that night. At a quarter to eight we were all assembled at the portal, still not quite believing our luck. But it was true enough. Promptly at eight a battered old car drove up and a few minutes later we were actually under way.

The soldier who did the driving proved to be delighted with

his mission. "The lieutenant told me about you people last night," he said proudly. "I think bringing you home is the nicest job I'll ever get in the Army." He drove fast and competently, with Nell in the front seat and the rest of us in the back, all strangely silent and tense, looking out at the familiar flat countryside around us and sadly noting the destruction in many of the towns and villages. The soldier at the wheel kept up a running commentary, telling us where the worst of the fighting had been, how the Allied armies had moved up, and the whole sad story of the unsuccessful parachute attack on Arnhem. After about an hour he asked, "Did any of you have breakfast this morning?"

We had to admit that we hadn't. For once, none of us had been hungry, and we had been too afraid of missing our rendezvous to take the chance of having to wait in the food line.

"I thought so," said our driver. "You're all pretty nervous, eh? Well, I brought you a big thermos of coffee. Why don't you pass that around? And I've some bars of chocolate in case you get hungry."

We gratefully drank the coffee and relaxed a little, but we couldn't eat. We were approaching the rivers now, and several big trucks were ahead of us on the road. "Now keep your fingers crossed," said the soldier. "Sometimes you have to wait for hours here, because all those big food trucks keep coming from all directions and every single one of them has to cross here and nowhere else."

But our luck held. There were only five trucks standing at the Meuse crossing, having their papers checked by a sentry; as our driver got out to show his papers, we watched them inching one by one over the makeshift bridge that looked as if it consisted solely of wooden planks and a few strands of wire. But, miraculously, it held. The soldier came back, and, in our turn, we crept over to the other bank.

"Had any trouble with those secret orders?" I asked our driver.

"None whatsoever," he replied cheerfully. "The lieutenant fixed them up fine."

I started to laugh. "Seems to me that all we've needed on this trip were some highly dubious papers," I said.

This, of course, had to be explained. We told our driver the story of the Russian passport that we couldn't read and of the phony document that had served us to get on the plane. He was delighted, and now asked more questions about how we had arrived in Oudenbosch; by the time we had crossed the Waal (a branch of the Rhine) and then the Rhine, we were chatting back and forth like old friends.

Then the moment had come for Dries to leave us and continue on his own. "Don't worry," said the soldier, after stopping the car at a strategic point. He shook Dries's hand "There's plenty of Canadian traffic along this road and nobody will refuse you a ride. Everybody hitch-hikes in Holland nowadays; it's the only way to get around."

We passed him his rucksack and he kissed his girls soundly.

"Oh, Dries," said Joke tremulously, "I do hope your mother is all right!"

"Write and let us know as soon as you can, will you?" urged Nell. My throat was suddenly so constricted that I couldn't bring out a word. I just kissed him and we left him standing there at the side of the road, a brave smile on his face and tears in his eyes. "His only family is his mother," Nell explained to the driver.

Joke was next. For the half-hour before we arrived at her home, she clutched her rucksack and sat stiffly upright in the back seat, too nervous to give comprehensible directions to the driver. When we stopped at the garden gate of her house, she was out of the car in a flash and dashing over the flagstone walk. Tensely, we waited in the car. The house looked all right; would her family be all right too? And then Joke and her mother came running out of the house together, and a great sigh of relief went up from all of us. Joke was dancing wildly around the car, laughing and crying at the same time. "Everybody is alive," she shouted. "Everybody, my daddy and my mother and my brothers! Everybody is alive!"

Her mother had opened the car door, and was leaning in, telling us excitedly that she had just corresponded with Nell's father (with whom Nell lived in Alkmaar) and that he was alive and well and eagerly awaiting her return.

"He knows then? He knows?" asked Nell unbelievingly.

"Of course he does!" cried Joke's mother. "We all knew. There was the letter to the Roosenburgs, the letter that came from England and said you were on your way."

So the Tommy from Riesa had mailed my letter![1] This was wonderful news indeed, especially for Nell, who could now relax and be sure that her father would be waiting for her. Joke was still dancing around, shouting her joyful message to the sky, the birds, and anybody who would listen. Her mother was urging us to come in and have something to eat. "Tell me," I interrupted her, "did you get in touch with Dries's mother?"

"Oh, yes," she answered, "she's all right too. Her house was bombed and we had some trouble locating her, because she had moved in with a sister or something. Wait a minute, I've got the letter here." She searched in the pockets of her skirts, but, not finding it, added desperately, "Oh, no, I haven't. It must be lying on the table. Won't you please come in for a minute?"

But she had already told us the most important things in our lives, and we suddenly remembered that our driver had to get back that same night.

Nell was beaming with happiness. "Just to think that my old dad survived it all!" she said incredulously.

Then our driver spoke up. "Haven't cried since I was a small boy, but do you know, I really felt like crying just now," he said wonderingly.

We dropped Jos where the highway to Rotterdam turned off.

[1] I do not know the name of the Tommy, but if he ever reads this book, I want him to realise how grateful all of us are to him.

Calm as ever, Jos picked up his bundle, hugged Nell and me, shook the driver's hand and started to walk down the turn-off. "Jos!" I yelled after him, "let us know how you get on, will you?"

"I certainly will," he shouted back, "good luck to you both!" And then he moved off, a confident blond boy, with a long stride and a bundle slung over one shoulder.

Now it was my turn. Like Joke, I sat clutching my bundles long before we arrived, but my tension translated itself into an urgent desire to talk. I gave the driver so many directions that he finally told me with a laugh, "Relax, will you? I know where you live now. I could get you there with my eyes closed." Then I repeated with Nell all the arrangements we had already made in Brussels, about who was going to write to which family about the imminent return of son, father, or sweetheart for all the skippers and Northerners we had left in Dessau. Nell patiently went over the whole list with me, apparently understanding that I had to talk about something to keep from exploding.

All of a sudden we were there. The car had swerved into my old street and pulled up in front of my old house. Hastily, I kissed Nell and thanked the soldier. I had told them not to wait, for we already knew that my family was all right and they would only lose precious time.

The front door was open, and a pail of water and a mop were standing just inside, evidence of the fact that our char-woman was there, scrubbing the premises in her usual vigorous manner. I could hear her moving around in the kitchen, and quickly dashed up the stairs before she could catch hold of me. Breathlessly, I burst into my father's study. He was standing there, holding a stethoscope to the chest of a half-undressed elderly man. I had forgotten that this was the doctor's consultation hour!

Dad dropped the stethoscope and we rushed into each other's arms. "My child, my child!" he repeated in an oddly high voice, as I sobbed wordlessly against his shoulder. Then suddenly he was tugging at my arm, saying, "Your mother was going out this afternoon, but maybe she hasn't left yet. We'd better go upstairs quick. Maybe she's still here."

Together we ran out of the room, leaving the poor, bewildered patient sitting on his chair, and climbed the stairs to the next floor three at a time. We ran smack into one of my sisters and, right on the top of the staircase, we teetered in a three-way embrace that might have toppled us all down if luck hadn't been with us. But finally my sister told us that mother had left about twenty minutes ago. "Every day since that letter came from England, she has refused to leave the house, waiting for you," my sister said almost accusingly, "and just today her friends persuaded her to take a little time off and come over for a visit and a game of bridge." Then she brightened and said, "But I know where she is, and its another doctor's home, so the phone will be working. I'm going to call right away!" She hurried away and my father and I were still clinging to each other at the top of the stairs.

"Dad, didn't you have a patient down there?" I stammered.

He slapped his forehead and said, "So I did. Wait till I get rid of him." With that he ran down the stairs like a young boy.

My sister emerged from my parents' bedroom and reported, "I got those people on the phone. Mother hadn't arrived yet, but they'll send her back as soon as she does. Oh, it's so good to have you back!" And again she was embracing me and I could feel her tears running down my neck.

All at once I became practical again. "Look," I said softly. "I brought some presents home. Let's arrange them nicely for mother, shall we?"

Together we went down to the living-room and arranged all the tinned goods I had brought from Belgium, the prison napkins, and my various prison embroideries on the coffee-table in front of the couch. Then Dad bounced in and said, "Right, I got rid of my patient. Now let's raise the flag. We've had it ready ever since we got that letter from England saying you were on your way. And we've got good news about your brother, too. Somebody came to tell us that he was alive two days after the camp was liberated, so he's probably on his way home."

Somehow the three of us managed to raise the flag, and the proud red, white and blue started to flap lazily in the gentle June breeze. It was June 13, 1945—five weeks since we had been liberated from Waldheim prison.

By the time my mother came bursting into the living-room, her arms stretched wide open, the three of us, my father, my sister, and I, were sitting rather stiffly on the couch behind my display of gifts. Physically they were in worse shape than I. All they had had to live on during the last months of the War was beet roots and tulip bulbs. I had learned, too, that my youngest sister was working in a hospital in Haarlem, but that dad would try to get her home on an emergency pass for the next week-end. At that point we ran out of words. None of us could express any of the feelings we had. But my mother broke the log jam. After we had cried for five minutes in each others' arms, she started asking so many questions that my father's and sister's tongues got untied too, and I soon found myself answering questions from all directions. Mother remained supremely indifferent to my Belgian gifts. "I've got you back," she repeated over and over, "I've got you back!"

Finally I picked up the small square of cotton that I had cut out of my prison underwear and embroidered in a spider-web pattern. "Look," I said proudly, "I made this specially for you. Will you keep it as a souvenir?"

At this point mother broke down again. "You couldn't have done this," she sobbed, "you never even knew in which hand to hold a needle."

Common Reader Editions

As booksellers since 1986, we have been stocking the pages of our monthly catalogue, A COMMON READER, with "Books for Readers with Imagination." Now as publishers, the same motto guides our work. Simply put, the titles we issue as COMMON READER EDITIONS are volumes of uncommon merit which we have enjoyed, and which we think other imaginative readers will enjoy as well. While our selections are as personal as the act of reading itself, what's common to our enterprise is the sense of shared experience a good book brings to solitary readers. We invite you to sample the wide range of COMMON READER EDITIONS, and welcome your comments.

commonreader.com